Teaching Chinese as a Foreign Language:
Chinese for Daily Conversations

对外汉语教程：基础日常用语

主编　杨海峰　陶玲　李永春

WUHAN UNIVERSITY PRESS
武汉大学出版社

图书在版编目(CIP)数据

对外汉语教程:基础日常用语/杨海峰,陶玲,李永春主编. —武汉:武汉
大学出版社,2024.12

ISBN 978-7-307-23506-9

Ⅰ.对… Ⅱ.①杨… ②陶… ③李… Ⅲ.汉语—口语—对外汉语
教学—教材 Ⅳ.H195.4

中国版本图书馆 CIP 数据核字(2022)第 248436 号

责任编辑:胡 艳 责任校对:李孟潇 版式设计:马 佳

出版发行:**武汉大学出版社** (430072 武昌 珞珈山)
(电子邮箱:cbs22@ whu.edu.cn 网址:www.wdp.com.cn)
印刷:武汉邮科印务有限公司
开本:787×1092 1/16 印张:15.25 字数:352 千字 插页:1
版次:2024 年 12 月第 1 版 2024 年 12 月第 1 次印刷
ISBN 978-7-307-23506-9 定价:48.00 元

前　言

本书以"针对性+实用性+知识性+趣味性"四位一体的原则，将对外汉语教学的语法翻译法、听说法、视听法、认知法、自觉对比法、功能法以及任务式教学法等有效结合，通过语言实用交际性提升学生学习动力，以语言对比分析提升学生理性认知，以趣味性和文化性营造轻松学习氛围，减少学生汉语学习过程中的文化过滤，使学生更好地掌握汉语语音、词汇、语法、文字知识，以及汉语听、说、读、写全方位语言技能。本书适用于零起点的汉语初学者。

【本教材的特点】

1. 注重听、说、读、写综合能力培养，特别加入了汉字造字法以及初文形体解说等内容，有助于学生对汉字的理解与学习；

2. 公众号平台"对外汉语教程：基础日常用语"配合教学，通过微视频，将课文及语法知识点演示出来；

3. 课文内容紧紧围绕《高等学校外国留学生汉语教学大纲》(2002)和留学生实际生活需求，词汇选取上，增加了"微信""支付宝""淘宝""京东""网购""快递"等使用频率较高、与学生学习生活联系密切的词汇。

【本教材的体例】

☞ 课文

1. 课文简短精练。本教材贯彻精讲多练原则，适用对象为汉语初学者，每篇课文设置内容简短。课文一般分成三部分：第一、二部分为分场景的简短对话，第三部分是对前两部分中段落的表述。课文第一、二部分旨在锻炼学生的对话交际能力，第三部分旨在提升学生的汉语语段表述能力。

课文未标注拼音，一方面是由于课文简短精练，难度可控；另一方面旨在锻炼学生对将汉语语音和汉字字形直接关联的能力，为此，我们从拉丁字母与汉字的对比出发，进行了符合汉字表意性特质的编排。

2. 注重交际功能。根据现代日常汉语实际使用情况，教材编排体现出时代性和实用性教学主题。每5课构成一个学习单元，并形成一个小的主题，学生在完成一个单元的学习后，可以就相关问题形成一个小的论述。如1~5课分别是："你叫什么名字？""你是哪国人？""你今年多大？""你学什么专业？""你为什么来中国留学？"这5篇课文形成的主题就是"自我介绍"，是留学生来中国学习必须要学会的交际用语。学完这5课，学生能够比较完整地介绍自己的姓名、国籍、年龄、专业以及来中国学习的目的，从而提升语言学习的实用价值。

☞ 词汇

1. 收录原则。教材根据现代汉语实际使用情况以及留学生汉语词汇教学大纲，收录了符合现代汉语交际情况、代表最新语言生活、符合词汇大纲要求掌握的重要词汇。

2. 词语展示。采取分类展示法，如分为名词、动词、形容词等进行分类展示，这符合范畴化认知规律，有助于提升学生识记效率。

3. 词意解释。采取拼音、英文、中文常见词组结合的方式。很多单音节词只有在组合时才能更明确意义，因此本教材在一般的拼音、英文注释基础上，加上了常见中文词组，有助于学生对词语意义的理解。

☞ 汉字

本教材注重学生听、说、读、写能力的全面培养，从汉语表意性特质出发，加强了汉字的理论介绍与字形的讲解。

1. 增加字形解说。如示出甲骨文等，帮助学生理解汉字的意义和演变，学习今天大多看起来无法解释的汉字在造字之初是如何理解的，帮助学生理解词义以及汉字字形的演变。

2. 展示汉字的结构和笔画。分析独体汉字和合体汉字，分析合体字的上下、左右、全包围等结构，展示每个汉字的笔画及笔顺。目的是从一开始学习，学生就培养汉字理性觉知能力，促进汉语学习成效。如：

独体字 single character　月　yuè　4画　

Its oracle script is , it is a pictograph character and it looks like the shape of the crescent moon. Its primitive sense is the moon.

☞ **注释**

这部分既包括语言知识的讲解，也包括文化民俗等方面内容的介绍。也就是说，除注重语法讲解外，本教材还加入了相应的汉字历史、汉语俗语以及中国文化等内容的介绍。对一种文化感兴趣往往能激发学生学习目的语的兴趣。文化渗入是缩短留学生与目的语社会的心理距离、加速文化适应的重要手段。汉字及汉语知识的讲解有助于留学生理性地语言学习，也就是在理解基础上的语言学习，这也符合成人学习第二语言的规律。因此，介绍语言背景的文化可以使课堂更加人性化和丰富多彩，使语言学习更加轻松愉悦，有助于指导留学生实际语言交际。

在文化注释部分，采用中英文讲解，让学生更易理解。

☞ **练习**

1. 原则：听、说、读、写综合训练，先听、说，后读、写，形式丰富有趣。

2. 听、说：生词部分的听、说训练，以图片与生词对应、汉语生词与英语释义对应、肢体表演汉语单词等形式展开。课文句子的听、说训练，以对话练习和自我展示、表演为主。

课文和生词音频

3. 读、写：读的训练可以引申一段与课文相关且包含此课生词的段落，让学生阅读和回答问题。写的训练分为：

(1)词语书写：把课文中考查的词语以填空的方式进行书写；

(2)汉字书写：展示甲骨文及对应汉字；画出汉字结构；写出汉字构成部件(合体字)，写出汉字笔画(独体字)；

(3)段落书写：用学到的词语及课文，自己写作一个小段落。

本教材是国家社会科学基金项目(21BYY138)、教育部基金项目(23YJC740034)、中央高校基本科研业务费专项资金(2017VI054、2022VI006-02)、东北石油大学 2022 年研究生教学改革项目(JGXM_NEPU_202115)、教育部高等教育司产学合作协同育人项目(221006642125730)、世界汉语教学学会全球中文教育主题学术活动计划(SH23Y38)以及2023 年湖北本科高校省级教学改革研究项目"机器人型信息终端与汉语国际教育教学的深度融合研究与实践"(2023111)等项目的成果之一。

汉语词类简称表
Word Class Abbreviations

简　称	英文名称	中文名称	拼　音
n	noun	名词	míngcí
pron	pronoun	代词	dàicí
num	numeral	数词	shùcí
quant	quantifier	量词	liàngcí
v	verb	动词	dòngcí
part	particle	助词	zhùcí
aux	auxiliary	助动词	zhùdòngcí
adj	adjective	形容词	xíngróngcí
adv	adverb	副词	fùcí
prep	preposition	介词	jiècí
conj	conjunction	连词	liáncí
ono	onomatopoeia	象声词	xiàngshēngcí
interj	interjection	叹词	tàncí
phr	phrase	短语	duǎnyǔ

课堂用语
Classroom Chinese

☞ 教师课堂用语 Classroom Chinese for Teacher

中 文	英 文	拼 音
同学们好！现在上课。	Hello, students! Now, let's begin our class.	Tóngxuémen hǎo! Xiànzài shàng kè.
请看黑板！	Please look at the blackboard!	Qǐng kàn hēibǎn!
请听我发音！	Please listen to my pronunciation!	Qǐng tīng wǒ fā yīn!
听我说。	Listen to me.	Tīng wǒ shuō.
跟我说。	Follow me to speak.	Gēn wǒ shuō.
跟我读。	Follow me to read.	Gēn wǒ dú.
跟我写。	Follow me to write.	Gēn wǒ xiě.
再听一遍。	Listen again.	Zài tīng yí biàn.
再读一遍。	Read again.	Zài dú yí biàn.
再说一遍。	Speak again.	Zài shuō yí biàn.
再写一遍。	Write again.	Zài xiě yí biàn.
现在听写。	Dictate now.	Xiànzài tīngxiě.
请打开书，翻到第( )页。	Please open the book and turn to ( ) page.	Qǐng dǎkāi shū, fāndào dì ( ) yè.
读课文，要大声朗读。	Read the text aloud.	Dú kèwén, yào dà shēng lǎngdú.
有问题请问。	If you have any questions, please ask.	Yǒu wèntí qǐng wèn.
现在布置作业。	Assign homework now.	Xiànzài bùzhì zuòyè.

续表

中　文	英　文	拼　音
预习新课的生词，要会读会写。	Preview the new vocabulary of the new lesson, you must know how to read and write.	Yùxí xīn kè de shēngcí, yào huì dú huì xiě.
请看一下语法/注释！	Please take a look at the grammar/notes!	Qǐng kàn yíxià yǔfǎ/zhùshì!
请把作业交给我！	Please give me the homework!	Qǐng bǎ zuòyè jiāo gěi wǒ!
下课。	Class is over.	Xià kè.

☞ 学生课堂用语 Classroom Chinese for Student

中　文	英　文	拼　音
老师好！	Hello, teacher!	Lǎoshī hǎo!
请您再慢一点儿！	Please slow down!	Qǐng nín zài màn yìdiǎner!
请您再说一遍！	Please repeat it again!	Qǐng nín zài shuō yí biàn!
请您再念一遍！	Please read it again!	Qǐng nín zài niàn yí biàn!
这个字/词怎么读？	How to pronounce this character/phrase?	Zhège zì/cí zěnme dú?
这个词是什么意思？	What does this word mean?	Zhège cí shì shénme yìsi?
英语的"——"汉语怎么说？	How do you say the English "——" in Chinese?	Yīngyǔ de"——"zěnme shuō?
今天的作业是什么？	What is today's homework?	Jīntiān de zuòyè shì shénme?
老师，他/她病了，不能来上课。	Teacher, he/she is sick and cannot come to class.	Lǎoshī, tā bìng le, bù néng lái shàng kè.
对不起，我迟到了。	Sorry, I'm late.	Duìbuqǐ, wǒ chídào le.
谢谢老师！	Thank you, teacher!	Xièxiè, lǎoshī!
再见！	Goodbye!	Zàijiàn!

目　　录

入门单元

Starter Unit ·· 1

　语音 Phonetics ·· 1

　练习 Exercises ··· 14

第一课　你叫什么名字?

Lesson 1　What's your name? ··· 17

　课文 Text ·· 17

　生词 New Words ·· 18

　汉字 Chinese Characters ·· 20

　注释 Notes ·· 23

　语法 Grammar ··· 24

　练习 Exercises ··· 25

第二课　你是哪国人?

Lesson 2　Which country are you from? ··· 28

　课文 Text ·· 28

　生词 New Words ·· 29

　汉字 Chinese Characters ·· 30

　注释 Notes ·· 31

　语法 Grammar ··· 32

　练习 Exercises ··· 33

第三课　你今年多大?

Lesson 3　How old are you? ································· 36

　　课文 Text ··· 36

　　生词 New Words ······································· 37

　　汉字 Chinese Characters ····························· 39

　　注释 Notes ··· 41

　　语法 Grammar ·· 42

　　练习 Exercises ······································· 44

第四课　你学什么专业?

Lesson 4　What's your major? ·························· 47

　　课文 Text ··· 47

　　生词 New Words ······································· 48

　　汉字 Chinese Characters ····························· 49

　　注释 Notes ··· 51

　　语法 Grammar ·· 52

　　练习 Exercises ······································· 53

第五课　你为什么来中国留学?

Lesson 5　Why did you come to study in China? ········· 56

　　课文 Text ··· 56

　　生词 New Words ······································· 57

　　汉字 Chinese Characters ····························· 58

　　语法 Grammar ·· 60

　　练习 Exercises ······································· 61

第六课　天气怎么样?

Lesson 6　What's the weather like? ····················· 64

　　课文 Text ··· 64

　　生词 New Words ······································· 65

　　汉字 Chinese Characters ····························· 67

　　语法 Grammar ·· 69

练习 Exercises ·· 70

第七课　现在几点?

Lesson 7　What time is it? ···················· 74

　　课文 Text ·· 74

　　生词 New Words ·································· 75

　　汉字 Chinese Characters ························ 77

　　注释 Notes ·· 80

　　语法 Grammar ···································· 80

　　练习 Exercises ···································· 81

第八课　今天星期几?

Lesson 8　What day is it today? ················ 84

　　课文 Text ·· 84

　　生词 New Words ·································· 85

　　汉字 Chinese Characters ························ 86

　　注释 Notes ·· 88

　　语法 Grammar ···································· 90

　　练习 Exercises ···································· 90

第九课　你去哪儿?

Lesson 9　Where are you going? ················ 93

　　课文 Text ·· 93

　　生词 New Words ·································· 94

　　汉字 Chinese Characters ························ 96

　　注释 Notes ·· 99

　　语法 Grammar ···································· 100

　　练习 Exercises ···································· 101

第十课　你在干什么?

Lesson 10　What are you doing? ················ 104

　　课文 Text ·· 104

生词 New Words ·· 105

汉字 Chinese Characters ·· 107

注释 Notes ··· 109

语法 Grammar ·· 111

练习 Exercises ··· 112

第十一课　这件衣服怎么样？

Lesson 11　How about this dress? ························· 115

课文 Text ··· 115

生词 New Words ·· 116

汉字 Chinese Characters ·· 118

语法 Grammar ·· 120

练习 Exercises ··· 121

第十二课　这件衣服多少钱？

Lesson 12　How much is this dress? ····················· 124

课文 Text ··· 124

生词 New Words ·· 125

汉字 Chinese Characters ·· 126

注释 Notes ··· 128

语法 Grammar ·· 130

练习 Exercises ··· 130

第十三课　怎样支付？

Lesson 13　How to pay? ····································· 134

课文 Text ··· 134

生词 New Words ·· 135

汉字 Chinese Characters ·· 136

语法 Grammar ·· 138

练习 Exercises ··· 139

第十四课　你会网购吗？

Lesson 14　Do you shop online？ ···················· 143

课文 Text ·················· 143

生词 New Words ·················· 144

汉字 Chinese Characters ·················· 147

语法 Grammar ·················· 149

练习 Exercises ·················· 150

第十五课　怎么取快递？

Lesson 15　How can I get the package？ ·················· 154

课文 Text ·················· 154

生词 New Words ·················· 155

汉字 Chinese Characters ·················· 157

注释 Notes ·················· 159

语法 Grammar ·················· 159

练习 Exercises ·················· 160

第十六课　为什么没来上课？

Lesson 16　Why aren't you in class？ ·················· 163

课文 Text ·················· 163

生词 New Words ·················· 164

汉字 Chinese Characters ·················· 166

语法 Grammar ·················· 168

练习 Exercises ·················· 169

第十七课　学了多长时间汉语？

Lesson 17　How long have you been learning Chinese？ ·················· 172

课文 Text ·················· 172

生词 New Words ·················· 173

汉字 Chinese Characters ·················· 175

注释 Notes ·················· 177

语法 Grammar ·················· 177

练习 Exercises ·························· 178

第十八课　你汉语说得怎么样？

Lesson 18　How is your spoken Chinese? ·········· 182

　课文 Text ·························· 182

　生词 New Words ·························· 183

　汉字 Chinese Characters ·········· 185

　语法 Grammar ·························· 187

　练习 Exercises ·························· 188

第十九课　考试难不难？

Lesson 19　Is the exam difficult? ·········· 191

　课文 Text ·························· 191

　生词 New Words ·························· 192

　汉字 Chinese Characters ·········· 194

　语法 Grammar ·························· 196

　练习 Exercises ·························· 197

第二十课　你什么时候回国？

Lesson 20　When will you return to your country? ·········· 201

　课文 Text ·························· 201

　生词 New Words ·························· 203

　汉字 Chinese Characters ·········· 205

　语法 Grammar ·························· 207

　练习 Exercises ·························· 208

生词索引表 ·························· 212

参考文献 ·························· 229

入门单元
Starter Unit

📅 语音 Phonetics

语音 Phonetics（1）

1. 音节 Formation of Chinese syllable

汉语的音节大多数由声母、韵母和声调组成，例如：bā、pá、mǎ、fà 都是音节。音节开头的辅音叫声母，例如：b、p、m、f。其余的部分是韵母，例如：ā、á、ǎ、à。现代汉语普通话有 400 多个音节。

Most Chinese syllables are formed by a combination of the initials, finals and tones. For example, bā, pá, mǎ, fà. The consonants at the head of a syllable（b, p, m, f in the above examples）are called the initials. The rest of the syllable is the final（ā、á、ǎ、à）. The contemporary Chinese Putonghua has over 400 syllables.

2. 声调 Tones

汉语普通话有四个基本声调，分别用声调符号：一声（ˉ）、二声（ˊ）、三声（ˇ）、四声（ˋ）。声调不同，表达的意思不同。例如：

Mandarin Chinese Putonghua has four basic tones. They are shown by the tone-marks：the 1st tone（ˉ）, the 2nd tone（ˊ）、the 3rd tone（ˇ）、the 4th tone（ˋ）. Different tones may express different meanings, e. g.

bā	bá	bǎ	bà
八	拔	靶	爸
eight	pull	target	dad

mā	má	mǎ	mà
妈	麻	马	骂
mum	numb	horse	scold

3. 变调　Modified tone

上声"ˇ"的变调　The modulations of "ˇ"

两个第三声音节连读时，前一个要读成第二声。例如：

When a 3rd tone is immediately followed by another 3rd tone, the former is pronounced as the 2nd tone, e.g.

ˇ	+	ˇ	⇨	´	+	ˇ
nǐ 你		hǎo 好		ní		hǎo
měi 美		hǎo 好		méi		hǎo
kě 可		yǐ 以		ké		yǐ

"不"的变调　The modulation of "不"

（1）"不"的本调是第四声：不 bù。

The original tone of 不 is the fourth tone bù.

（2）"不"在第一、二、三声前声调不变，仍然读第四声。

The tone of "不" remains unchanged before the first, second and third tones syllables.

（3）"不"在第四声音节前边时，变为第二声。

When "不" is in front of the fourth tone syllable, it becomes the second tone bú.

不　　bù			不　　bú
不　+　一声	不　+　二声	不　+　三声	不　+　四声
bù　　chī 不　　吃	bù　　lái 不　　来	bù　　zǒu 不　　走	bú　　qù 不　　去
bù　　hē 不　　喝	bù　　xíng 不　　行	bù　　hǎo 不　　好	bú　　shì 不　　是

"一"的变调 The modulation of "一"

（1）"一"的本调是第一声：一 yī，例如表示数字和顺序：一、第一。

The original tone of 一 is the first tone yī, e.g. 一 (one); 第一 (the first).

（2）"一"在第一声、第二声、第三声音节前边时，变为第四声。

When "一" is in front of the first, second and third tone syllables, it becomes the fourth tone yì.

（3）"一"在第四声音节前边时，变为第二声。

When "一" is in front of the fourth tone syllable, it becomes the second tone yí.

一　　yì			一　　yí
一　+　一声	一　+　二声	一　+　三声	一　+　四声
yì　　tiān 一　　天	yì　　huí 一　　回	yì　　bǎ 一　　把	yí　　jiàn 一　　件

4. 轻声 Chinese neutral tone

轻声是一种特殊的变调现象。由于它长期处于口语轻读音节的地位，失去了原有声调的调值，又重新构成自身特有的音高形式，听感上显得轻短模糊。

Chinese neutral tone is a special kind of pitch-shifting phenomenon. Because it has been in the position of light reading syllables in spoken language for a long time, it has lost the tone value of the original tone, and has reconstituted its own unique pitch form, which makes it appear light, short and vague in listening sense.

3

轻声作为一种变调的语音现象，一定体现在词语和句子中，因此轻声音节的读音不能独立存在。

As a tone-changing phonetic phenomenon, neutral tones must be reflected in words and sentences, so the pronunciation of neutral tones cannot exist independently.

例如，"爸爸""妈妈""喇叭""枕头"，第二个字都读轻声。

e.g. "Dad""Mother""Trumpet""Pillow", the second word is read softly.

爸爸 bàba　　　妈妈 māma

喇叭 lǎba　　　枕头 zhěntou

名词词尾"子"也都读轻声。例如：

The noun ending "子" is also read softly, e.g.

饺子 jiǎozi　　　肉包子 ròubāozi　　　椅子 yǐzi

5. 儿化　Retroflex suffixation

特殊韵母 er 同其他韵母合成一个音节，使这个韵母变为卷舌韵母的语言现象，叫做儿化。儿化了的韵母就叫"儿化韵"，其标志是在韵母后面加上"r"。儿化后的字音仍是一个音节。例如：

The special final er is combined with other finals to synthesize a syllable, so that this final becomes a language phenomenon of a tongue-rolling final. This phenomenon is called retroflex final which is marked by adding er after the final. The sound of the word with retroflex final is still a syllable. e. g.

画儿 huàr　　　哪儿 nǎr　　　玩儿 wánr

小孩儿 xiǎoháir　　　一对儿 yíduìr　　　小曲儿 xiǎoqǔr

语音　Phonetics（2）

1. 声母　Initials

普通话共有21个辅音声母，根据发音部位不同，可分为双唇音、唇齿音、舌尖中音、舌根音、舌面音、舌尖前音、舌尖后音七类。有送气音和不送气音区别和卷舌音的特点。

There are 21 consonant initials in Mandarin Chinese, which can be divided into seven categories: bilabial, labiodental, mid-tongue, root, face, front and back. There are characteristics of the difference between aspirated and unaspirated sounds and reflexes.

b　p　m　（双唇音　Bilabial）

b 双唇无气破裂音，**p** 和 **b** 发音相对立，是送气音。**m** 双唇紧闭，软腭、小舌下垂，气流从鼻腔出来。例如：

b There is no breathless cracking of the lips, and the pronunciation of **p** is opposite, which is an aspiration sound. **m** The lips are tightly closed, the soft palate and uvula are drooping, and the air flows out of the nasal cavity, e.g.

爸爸 bàba　皮包 píbāo　妈妈 māma

f　（唇齿音　Labiodental）

f 上齿接触下唇，气流从中间摩擦而出。例如：

f The upper teeth touch the lower lip, and the airflow rubs out from the middle, e.g.

米饭 mǐfàn　反复 fǎnfù　夫妇 fūfù

d　t　n　l　（舌尖中音　Alto on the tip of the tongue）

d 舌尖中不送气破裂音。**t** 舌尖中送气破裂音。**n** 舌尖顶上齿龈、软腭，小舌下垂，鼻腔共鸣发音。

d The unaspirated plosive of the tip of the tongue.

t The aspirated plosive of the tip of the tongue.

n The gums and soft palate on the top of the tongue, the uvula droops, and the nasal cavity resonates.

l 舌尖顶上齿龈，比 n 稍后，气流从舌前部两边出来。例如：

l The tip of the tongue is on the top of the gums, later than **n**, and the airflow comes out from both sides of the front of the tongue, e.g.

担担面 dàndanmiàn　　酸辣汤 suānlàtāng　　唐三彩 tángsāncǎi

g　k　h　（舌根音　Root sound）

g 不送气音，**k** 送气音。

h 舌根接近软腭，气流从中间摩擦而出。

g Unaspirated sound.

k Aspirated sound.

h The base of the tongue is close to the soft palate, and the air is rubbed out from the middle.

哈巴狗 hǎbagǒu　　　北京烤鸭 Běijīngkǎoyā　　　改革开放 gǎigé kāifàng

j　q　x （舌面音 Tongue and face）

j 不送气音，使舌面更宽广地发音。**q** 送气音，气流强烈摩擦而出。

x 舌面前部与硬腭相近，气流摩擦而出。

j Unaspirated sound, so that the tongue surface is more widely pronounced.

q Aspirating sound, the airflow is strongly rubbed out.

x The front part of the tongue is close to the hard palate, and the air rubs out.

经济学家 jīngjìxuéjiā　　　　琴棋书画 qín qí shū huà

选举 xuǎnjǔ　　　　　　　洗衣机 xǐyījī

z　c　s （舌尖前音 Tip of the tongue）

z 舌尖前阻，不送气，清塞擦音。发音时，舌尖平伸，顶上齿背，然后舌尖移开些，让气流从空腔中所留的空隙间摩擦出来。与 **z** 对应的是 **c**，要尽量送气。**s** 是舌尖接近下齿背，气流从舌面中缝跟上齿中间摩擦而出。

z The tip of the tongue is blocked forward, unaspirated, and clear affricate. When pronouncing, the tip of the tongue is stretched flat against the back of the teeth, and then the tip of the tongue is moved away to allow the air to rub out of the space left in the cavity. Corresponding to **z** is **c**, try to aspirate as much as possible.

s The tip of the tongue is close to the back of the lower teeth, and the air rubs out from the middle seam of the tongue surface and the middle of the upper teeth.

藏族 Zàngzú　　　曹操 Cáo cāo　　　朝三暮四 zhāo sān mù sì

自行车 zìxíngchē　　　瓷器 cíqì　　　　汽车司机 qìchē sījī

zh　ch　sh　r （舌尖后音 Back of tongue）

zh 舌尖后阻，不送气，清塞擦音。发音时舌尖上卷，顶住硬腭，气流从舌尖与硬腭间爆发摩擦而出。与 **zh** 对应的是 **ch**，但要送气。**sh** 是舌尖后阻，清擦音。舌尖上卷，接近硬腭，气流从舌尖与硬腭间摩擦而出。**zh** The tip of the tongue is obstructed backward, without aspirating, with a clear affricate. When pronouncing, the tip of the tongue rolls up and presses against the hard palate, and the airflow erupts from the friction between the tip of the tongue and the hard palate.

Corresponding to **zh** is **ch**, but with aspiration.

sh Voiceless post-alveolar affricate. The tip of the tongue is rolled up, close to the hard palate, and the air rubs out from the tip of the tongue and the hard palate.

r 舌尖后阻，浊擦音。发音部位与 **sh** 一样，但是浊音。中国东北地方的方言很多把 **r** 发成 **i**，要注意。

r After the tongue tip resistance, voiced fricative. The pronunciation part is the same as **sh**, but voiced. Many dialects in Northeast China pronounce **r** as **i**, so be careful.

赵先生 Zhào xiānsheng	张老师 Zhāng lǎoshī
陈女士 Chén nǚshì	中国 Zhōngguó
日本 Rìběn	如入无人之境 rú rù wú rén zhī jìng

2. 韵母　Finals

韵母是普通话音节中最重要的部分，由韵头、韵腹和韵尾组成。韵腹也叫主要元音，是韵母的核心。普通话共有 39 个韵母。

The finals is the most important part of a Mandarin Chinese syllable, and consists of a rhyme head, a rhyme belly and a rhyme tail. The rhyme belly is also called the main vowel and is the core of the final. There are 39 finals in Mandarin Chinese.

a　ai　ao　an　ang

a 开口度最大，舌位最低，唇不圆。例如：

a The opening is the largest, the tongue is the lowest, and the lips are not round, e.g.

巴拿马 Bānámǎ	加拿大 Jiānádà

ai 口腔稍微狭窄，边发 **a** 音，舌头边向前上方移动。例如：

ai The mouth is slightly narrow, and the tongue moves forward and upward while making the **a** sound, e.g.

来客 láikè	白色 báisè

ao 口腔扩大，边发 **a** 音，边使唇微圆。例如：

ao The mouth is enlarged, making the **a** sound while making the lips slightly rounded, e.g.

毛发 máofà	朝鲜 Cháoxiǎn

an 先发 **a**，舌位逐渐抬起，舌尖抵住上齿龈，软腭下降，嘴唇向两边展开，开口度稍小。例如：

an First attack **a**, the tongue is gradually raised, the tip of the tongue is against the upper gum, the soft palate is lowered, the lips are spread out to both sides, and the opening is slightly smaller, e.g.

丹麦 Dānmài   韩国 Hánguó

ang 先发 **a** 音，舌根抵住上软腭，气流从鼻腔泄出，发后鼻音尾 ng 的音。例如：

ang The sound of **a** is pronounced first, the base of the tongue touches the upper soft palate, the air is vented from the nasal cavity, and the sound of ng after the nasal end is pronounced, e.g.

长江 Chángjiāng   黄河 Huánghé

o ou ong

o 开口度中等，舌位半高、偏后，圆唇，和声母 **b**、**p**、**m**、**f** 结合。例如：

o The opening degree is medium, the tongue is half-high, slightly posterior, with round lips, combined with the initials **b**, **p**, **m**, **f**, e.g.

玻璃 bōli   佛教 fójiào

ou 先发 o 的音，嘴唇渐收拢，舌根抬高，口型由大圆到小圆。例如：

ou The sound of **o** is pronounced first, the lips are gradually drawn together, the base of the tongue is raised, and the mouth shape changes from big round to small round, e.g.

瘦肉 shòuròu   臭豆腐 chòudòufu

ong 先发 o 音，舌根后缩抵住软腭，舌面隆起，嘴唇拢圆，鼻腔共鸣成声。例如：

ong starts with the **o** sound, the base of the tongue is retracted against the soft palate, the tongue surface is raised, the lips are rounded, and the nasal cavity resonates into a sound, e.g.

空中 kōngzhōng   龙虎 lónghǔ

e ei en eng

e 开口度中等，舌位半高、偏后，唇不圆。例如：

e The mouth opening is moderate, the tongue is half-high and set back, and the lips are not round, e.g.

合格 hégé   客人 kèren

ei 先发 e 音，由 e 向 i 滑动，气流不中断，发音连续，音由强到弱。例如：

ei Make the sound of **e** first, slide from **e** to **i**, the airflow is not interrupted, the pronunciation is continuous, and the sound is from strong to weak, e.g.

谁 shéi   妹妹 mèimei

en 先发 e 的音，由 e 向 n 滑动，气流不中断，发音连续，音由强到弱。例如：

en Start with the sound of **e**, slide from **e** to **n**, the airflow is not interrupted，the pronunciation is continuous, and the sound changes from strong to weak，e.g.

森林 sēnlín   本人 běnrén

eng 先发 **e** 的音，由 **e** 向 **ng** 滑动发音。例如：

eng Start with the sound of **e**, then slide the sound from **e** to **ng**，e.g.

朋友 péngyou   长城 Chángchéng

er

er 不和声母结合，常常单独构成音节。发 **er** 时，先把舌位放置发 **e** 的位置，然后将舌尖轻轻上翘，同时发音。例如：

er is not combined with an initial, but often forms a syllable by itself. When pronouncing **er**, first place the tongue in the position where the pronouncing **e** is, and then lift the tip of the tongue slightly，and pronounce at the same time，e.g.

形而上学 xíng'érshàngxué   普洱茶 pǔ'ěrchá

i ia iao ian iang ie iou in ing iong

i 开口度最小，唇扁平，舌位高、偏前。不和声母结合，单独构成音节时是 **yi**。例如：

i The mouth opening is the smallest, the lips are flat, and the tongue is high and forward. It is **yi** when it is not combined with the initials and forms a syllable alone，e.g.

大米 dàmǐ   中医 zhōngyī

ia 嘴唇微张，由 **i** 滑动到 **a** 的位置，舌位由高位降到最低，舌面由前向中央移动，唇形逐渐转为大开。**i** 发音轻短，**a** 发音清晰响亮。不和声母结合，单独构成音节时是 **ya**。例如：

ia The lips are slightly opened, slide from **i** to the position of **a**, the tongue position is lowered from the high position to the lowest position，the tongue surface moves from the front to the center, and the lip shape gradually turns wide open. The i is short and light, and the a is clear and loud. It is **ya** when it is not combined with the initials and forms a syllable alone，e.g.

龙虾 lóngxiā   假牙 jiǎyá

iao 由 **i** 滑动到 **a** 及 **o** 的位置，舌位由高位降到低位，再升到半高位，舌头向前移动，唇形由扁平状到大开，最后成圆形。**i** 发音轻短，**a** 发音清亮，**o** 发音较模糊。不和声母结合，单独构成音节时是 **yao**。例如：

iao Slide from **i** to the positions of **a** and **o**, the tongue position drops from high to low, then rises to half-high, the tongue moves forward, the lip shape changes from flat to wide, and finally becomes round shape. **i** is short and light, **a** is clear, and **o** is vague. It is **yao** when it is not combined with the initials and forms a syllable alone, e.g.

缥缈 piāomiǎo   窈窕 yǎotiǎo

ian 舌尖抵下齿背，舌位由前高元音 **i** 处向半低元音 **a** 处落下，舌尖或舌面前部抬起与齿龈接触；阻塞气流，使声音和气息从鼻腔通过，发出前鼻尾复合音 **ian**。不和声母结合，单独构成音节时是 **yan**。例如：

ian The tip of the tongue touches the back of the lower teeth, the tongue falls from the front high vowel **i** to the semi-low vowel **a**, the tip of the tongue or the front part of the tongue is lifted to contact the gums; the airflow is blocked, so that the sound and breath pass through the nasal cavity and emit Anterior nasal tail compound sound ian. It is **yan** when it is not combined with the initials and forms a syllable alone, e.g.

缅甸 Miǎndiàn   语言 yǔyán

iang 先发轻短的韵头 **i**，然后滑动到韵腹 **a**，舌位由高降到最低，舌头后缩，软腭下降，舌根抵住软腭，气流从鼻腔通过，归音到舌根鼻辅音 **ng**。嘴唇展开，开口度由小稍转大。不和声母结合，单独构成音节时是 **yang**。例如：

iang First make a light and short rhyme **i**, then slide to the rhythm belly **a**, the tongue position is lowered from high to the lowest, the tongue is retracted, the soft palate is lowered, the base of the tongue is against the soft palate, the airflow passes through the nasal cavity, and the sound returns to the base of the tongue. **ng**. The lips are spread out, and the opening degree is changed from small to large. It is **yang** when it is not combined with the initials and forms a syllable alone, e.g.

香港 Xiānggǎng   绵羊 miányáng

ie 从 **i** 向 **e** 的状态滑动。不和声母结合，单独构成音节时是 **ye**。例如：

ie Swipe from **i** to **e** state. It is **ye** when it is not combined with the initials and forms a syllable alone, e.g.

姐姐 jiějie   爷爷 yéye

iou 从 **i** 向 **ou** 的状态滑动。不和声母结合，单独构成音节时是 **you**。例如：

iou Swipe from **i** to **ou** state. It is **you** when it is not combined with the initials and forms a syllable alone, e.g.

悠久 yōujiǔ   皮球 píqiú

in 从 **i** 向 **in** 的状态滑动。不和声母结合，单独构成音节时是 **yin**。例如：

in Swipe from **i** to **in** state. It is **yin** when it is not combined with the initials and forms a syllable alone，e.g.

天津 Tiānjīn　　　　　　　　印象 yìnxiàng

ing 从 **i** 向 **ng** 的状态滑动。不和声母结合，单独构成音节时是 **ying**。例如：

ing Swipe from the state of **i** to **ng**. It is **ying** when it is not combined with the initials and forms a syllable alone，e.g.

北京 Běijīng　　　　　　　　英语 Yīngyǔ

iong 从 **i** 向 **ong** 的状态滑动。不和声母结合，单独构成音节时是 **yong**。例如：

iong Swipe from **i** to **ong** state. It is **yong** when it is not combined with the initials and forms a syllable alone，e.g.

匈牙利 Xiōngyálì　　　　　　　游泳池 yóuyǒngchí

> **u ua uo uai uan uang uei uen ueng**

u 开口度最小，唇最圆，舌位高、偏后。不和声母结合，单独构成音节时是 **wu**。例如：

u The opening is the smallest, the lips are the most rounded, and the tongue is high and set back. It is **wu** when it is not combined with the initial consonant and forms a syllable alone，e.g.

老虎 lǎohǔ　　　　　　　　武器 wǔqì

ua 从 **u** 向 **a** 的状态滑动。不和声母结合，单独构成音节时是 **wa**。例如：

ua Swipe from the state of **u** to **a**. It is **wa** when it is not combined with the initials and forms a syllable alone，e.g.

中国话 Zhōngguóhuà　　　　　　娃娃 wáwa

uo 从 **u** 向 **o** 的状态滑动。不和声母结合，单独构成音节时是 **wo**。例如：

uo Swipe from **u** to **o**. It is **wo** when it is not combined with the initials and forms a syllable alone，e.g.

火锅 huǒguō　　　　　　　　我 wǒ

uai 从 **u** 向 **ai** 的状态滑动。不和声母结合，单独构成音节时是 **wai**。例如：

uai Swipe from **u** to **ai** state. It is **wai** when it is not combined with the initials and forms a syllable alone，e.g.

快车 kuàichē　　　　　　　　外语 wàiyǔ

uan 从 **u** 向 **an** 的状态滑动。不和声母结合，单独构成音节时是 **wan**。例如：

11

uan Swipe from the state of **u** to **an**. It is **wan** when it is not combined with the initials and forms a syllable alone，e.g.

酸辣汤 suānlàtāng   砂锅丸子 shāguōwánzi

uang 从 **u** 向 **ang** 的状态滑动。不和声母结合，单独构成音节时是 **wang**。例如：

uang Swipe from the state of **u** to **ang**. It is **wang** when it is not combined with the initials and forms a syllable alone，e.g.

广场 guǎngchǎng   网球 wǎngqiú

uei 从 **u** 向 **ei** 的状态滑动。不和声母结合，单独构成音节时是 **wei**。例如：

uei Swipe from **u** to **ei**. It is **wei** when it is not combined with the initials and forms a syllable alone，e.g.

挪威 Nuówēi   开水 kāishuǐ

uen 从 **u** 向 **en** 的状态滑动。不和声母结合，单独构成音节时是 **wen**。例如：

uen Swipe from **u** to **en** state. It is **wen** when it is not combined with the initials and forms a syllable alone，e.g.

文莱 Wénlái   温和 wēnhé

ueng 从 **u** 向 **eng** 的状态滑动。不和声母结合，单独构成音节时是 **weng**。例如：

ueng Swipe from **u** to **eng** state. It is **weng** when it is not combined with the initials and forms a syllable alone，e.g.

富翁 fùwēng

ü üe üan ün

ü 舌位与 **i** 相同，但要圆唇，口角用力。不和声母结合，单独构成音节时是 **yu**；和声母 **j**、**q**、**x** 结合时，**ü** 上面两点去掉，写成 **u**；和 **n**、**l** 结合时，仍写成 **ü**。这条规则也适用于 **üe**。例如：

ü The tongue position is the same as **i**, but the lips are rounded and the corners of the mouth are forced. When it is not combined with an initial, it is **yu** when it forms a syllable alone；when combined with an initial **j**，**q**，**x**, the two points above **ü** are removed and written as **u**；when combined with **n**，**l**, it is still written as **u**. This rule also applies to **üe**，e.g.

女律师 nǚlùshī   下雨 xià yǔ

üe 从 **ü** 向 **e** 的状态滑动，口型由圆到扁。不和声母结合，单独构成音节时是 **yue**。例如：

üe Slide from **ü** to **e**, and the mouth shape changes from round to flat. It is **yue** when it is not combined with the initials and forms a syllable alone，e.g.

省略 shěnglüè　　　　　　　音乐 yīnyuè

üan 从 **ü** 向 **an** 的状态滑动。不和声母结合，单独构成音节时是 **yuan**。例如：

üan Swipe from the state of **ü** to **an**. It is **yuan** when it is not combined with the initials and forms a syllable alone，e.g.

元旦 yuándàn　　　　　　　劝说 quànshuō

ün 从 **ü** 向 **n** 的状态滑动。不和声母结合，单独构成音节时是 **yun**。例如：

ün Swipe from the state of **ü** to **n**. It is **yun** when it is not combined with the initials and forms a syllable alone，e.g.

云南 Yúnnán　　　　　　　运动 yùndòng

3. 拼音　Initial-final combinations

	a	o	e	i	u	ü	ai	ei	ao	ou
b	ba	bo		bi	bu		bai	bei	bao	
p	pa	po		pi	pu		pai	pei	pao	pou
m	ma	mo	me	mi	mu		mai	mei	mao	mou
f	fa	fo			fu			fei		fou
d	da		de	di	du		dai	dei	dao	dou
t	ta		te	ti	tu		tai		tao	tou
n	na		ne	ni	nu	nü	nai	nei	nao	nou
l	la		le	li	lu	lü	lai	lei	lao	lou
g	ga		ge		gu		gai	gei	gao	gou
k	ka		ke		ku		kai	kei	kao	kou
h	ha		he		hu		hai	hei	hao	hou
				yi	wu	yu				

🔊 练习 Exercises

一、声调 Tones

1. 辨别声调 Identifying the tones

（1）ā　　á　　ǎ　　à

（2）ō　　ó　　ǒ　　ò

（3）ī　　í　　ǐ　　ì

（4）ū　　ú　　ǔ　　ù

（5）ǖ　　ǘ　　ǚ　　ǜ

2. 声调搭配 Tone matching

（1）bā　　bá　　bǎ　　bà

（2）mā　　má　　mǎ　　mà

（3）bū　　bú　　bǔ　　bù

（4）mī　　mí　　mǐ　　mì

（5）gōu　　góu　　gǒu　　gòu

二、轻声 Chinese neutral tone

（1）bàba　　　　māma　　　　yéye　　　　nǎinai

（2）gēzi　　　　yāzi　　　　duìle　　　　cuòle

（3）páopaotǔ　　　　zhuōzhuochóng

（4）xiǎngyixiǎng　　　　suànyisuàn

（5）guòleqiáo　　　　cāzhuōzi

三、儿化 Retroflex suffixation

进了门儿，倒杯水，喝了两口儿运运气儿，顺手拿起小唱本儿，唱一曲儿，又一曲儿，练完了嗓子我练嘴皮儿。绕口令儿，练字音儿，还有单弦儿牌子曲儿，小快板儿，大鼓词儿，越说越唱我越带劲儿。

四、辨音 Pronunciation exercises

1. 辨别声母 Identify the initials

（1）ba　　pa　　da　　ta　　ga　　ka

（2）bu　　pu　　du　　tu　　gu　　ku

（3）bai　　pai　　dai　　tai　　gai　　kai

（4）bao　　pao　　dao　　tao　　gao　　kao

2. 辨别韵母 Identify the finals

（1）ba　　　bo　　　bi　　　bu

（2）pa　　　po　　　pi　　　pu

（3）ma　　　mo　　　me　　　mi mu

（4）fa　　　fo　　　fu

（5）dai　　dei　　dao　　dou

（6）tai　　tao　　tou

（7）nai　　nei　　nao　　nou

3. 辨别声调 Identify tones

（1）bāi　　bái　　bǎi　　bài

（2）hēi　　héi　　hěi　　hèi

（3）tuī　　tuí　　tuǐ　　tuì

（4）diū　　diú　　diǔ　　diù

（5）hāo　　háo　　hǎo　　hào

五、认读 Read and learn

1. 认读拼音 Read the following Chinese phonetic alphabet

yíhào　　　yìbǎi　　　wǔhào　　　wǔbǎi

bāhào　　　dàmǎ　　　báimǎ　　　bùhǎo

dìtú　　　fādá　　　dàmén　　　gāolóu

2. 认读中国人的姓氏 Read the following Chinese surname

高 Gāo　　　孙 Sūn　　　周 Zhōu　　　张 Zhāng

王 Wáng　　　陈 Chén　　　徐 Xú　　　刘 Liú

李 Lǐ   蒋 Jiǎng   马 Mǎ   沈 Shěn

邓 Dèng   赵 Zhào   宋 Sòng   叶 Yè

3. **认读化学元素 Read the following chemical element**

汞（mercury）   gǒng   钨（tungsten）   wū   铂（platinum）   bó

砷（arsenic）   shēn   氮（nitrogen）   dàn   镁（magnesium）   měi

钙（calcium）   gài   氧（oxygen）   yǎng   氢（hydrogen）   qīng

六、绕口令 Tongue twister

吃葡萄

chī pútao

吃 葡 萄 不 吐 葡 萄 皮 儿，

chī pútao bù tǔ pútao pír,

不 吃 葡 萄 倒 吐 葡 萄 皮 儿。

bù chī pútao dǎo tǔ pútao pír.

第一课　你叫什么名字？
Lesson 1　What's your name?

📅 课文 Text

课文一　Text 1

在机场，中国学生一明和老师大江来接留学生大山和小米。大山、小米办完入境手续，到大厅后，看到写着"大山""小米"字样的牌子。

At the airport, Chinese Students Yi Ming and the teacher Mr. Da Jiang come to pick up the international students Da Shan and Xiao Mi. Dashan and Xiao Mi go through entry formalities. After arriving at the hall, they see a sign that says "Da Shan" "Xiao Mi".

（大山、小米朝牌子的方向走去。）

（Da Shan and Xiao Mi walk toward the direction of the sign.）

大山：你好，请问你叫什么名字？

一明：我叫一明，你叫大山吗？

大山：是的，我叫大山。

小米：你好，一明，我叫小米。

一明：你好，小米。

课文二　Text 2

（老师大江插话。）

（Mr. Da Jiang interjected.）

大江：你好，大山。

大山：您好，请问您怎么称呼？

大江：我叫大江，欢迎你们。

大山：谢谢！

小米：谢谢！

✍ 生词 New Words

生　词	词　性	解　释	举　例
你 nǐ	pron	you	你是谁？ Who are you?
叫 jiào	v	call sb's name	你叫大山。 You are Dashan.
什么 shénme	pron	what	这是什么？ What is this?
名字 míngzi	n	name	你叫什么名字？ What's your name?
好 hǎo	adj	good；fine；ok	这是一本好书。 This is a good book.
你好 nǐ hǎo		hello；how do you do	你好，一明！ Hello, Yi Ming!
请问 qǐng wèn		excuse me	请问体育馆怎么走？ Excuse me. How can I get to the gym?
吗 ma	part	used to express question at the end of straight sentence particle to indicate interrogative mood	你好吗？ How are you?
是 shì	interj	be（used to connect the subject of the sentence to its complement）	我是学生。 I am a student.

续表

生 词	词 性	解 释	举 例
的 de	part	is often added to declarative sentence expressing affirmative sentence	是的。 Yes. 好的。 Ok.
是的 shìde		yes	是的，我叫小米。 Yes, my name is Xiao Mi.
我 wǒ	pron	I；me	我叫大山。 I am Dashan.
您 nín	pron	the polite expression of "你"	您是张教授吗? Are you Prof. Zhang?
您好 nín hǎo		hello	老师您好! Hello, teacher!
怎么 zěnme	adv	how	这道题怎么解? How to solve this problem?
称呼 chēnghu	vt	call；name；address	您怎么称呼? What's your name?
欢迎 huānyíng	vt	welcome	欢迎你。 Welcome to you.
你们 nǐmen	pron	plural pronoun you	你们好! How do you do!
们 men	auxiliary word	used after a personal pronoun or a noun to show plural number	我们，你们，他们 we，you，they
谢谢 xièxie	vt	thanks；thank you	谢谢你的好意! Thank you for your kindness!

汉 汉字 Chinese Characters

独体字(dútǐzì)　　Single character

我

The shape evolution of 我 are as follows：

Its original meaning is an ancient weapon — a large axe with a row of sharp teeth. Its phonetic loaned sense is I me.

合体字(hétǐzì)　　Combined character

你　左右结构 zuǒyòu jiégòu　Left-right structure　　亻　尔

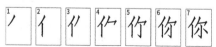

The left part 亻 is 人 (rén) which means a person, the right part is 尔 (ěr) which means you are in ancient Chinese.

好　左右结构 zuǒyòu jiégòu　Left-right structure　　女　子

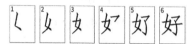

The left part is 女 (nǚ) which means female, the right part is 子 (zǐ), which means children in ancient Chinese. 好 means it's wonderful for women to have children. It is an ideograph.

请　左右结构 zuǒyòu jiégòu　Left-right structure　　讠　青

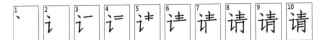

The left part is 讠(言 yán) which means speaking, the right part is

青(qīng) which means blue or green and it has the similar pronunciation as 请.

请 is a pictophonetic character which means ask for help or ask someone to do something

politely. It is a polite expression.

叫　左右结构 zuǒyòu jiégòu　Left-right structure　口　丩

The left part 口(kǒu) means mouth, the right part 丩(jiū) is the phonetic element, its

pronunciation is similar to 叫(jiào). 叫 is a signific-phonetic character.

称　左右结构 zuǒyòu jiégòu　Left-right structure　禾　尔

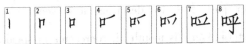

The ancient writing of 称 is 稱. The left part 禾(hé) means cereal plant. The right part

爯(chēng) means weighing and its pronunciation is the same as 稱. So 稱 is a signific-

phonetic character in ancient Chinese. Its modern simplified Chinese character is 称,

The right part is 尔(ěr), and 称 is not a signific-phonetic character.

呼　左右结构 zuǒyòu jiégòu　Left-right structure　口　乎

呼(hū) is composed by 口 and 乎(hū), it is a signific-phonetic character which

means to call or to shout, e.g. 称呼, 呼叫.

迎　左下包围结构 zuǒxià bāowéi jiégòu　Lower-left Surrounding structure　辶　卬

It is a signific-phonetic character. The signific element 辶(chuò) means walk. The

phonetic element 卬(yǎng) means hold (one's head) high and look up at sb/sth. Its pronunciation is similar to 迎. 迎 looks like sb. is happy and walks quickly to meet sb.

谢 左右结构 zuǒyòu jiégòu　Left-right structure　讠　射(身+寸)

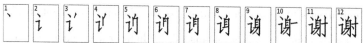

谢 is composed by 讠(言 yán) 和 射(shè). 讠 means speak and talk. In ancient Chinese the pronunciation 射 is similar to 谢(xiè), 谢 is a pictophonetic character.

吗 左右结构 zuǒyòu jiégòu　Left-right structure　口　马

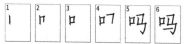

吗 is a signific-phonetic character. Its signific element is 口, and its phonetic element is 马(mǎ).

的 左右结构 zuǒyòu jiégòu　Left-right structure　白　勺

的 is composed by 白(bái) 和 勺(sháo).

名 上下结构 shàngxià jiégòu　Upper-lower structure　夕　口

Its oracle script is ♪. The upper part 夕(xī) describes a crescent moon which represents the night. The lower part 口(kǒu) is mouth, it represents to speak. It is an ideograph character which describes people can't see each other at night so they have to say their names out. Therefore its primitive sense is name.

是 上下结构 shàngxià jiégòu　Upper-lower structure　日　疋

The upper part is 日(rì) means the sun. The lower part 疋 is 正(zhèng) which means non-skew. 是 represents going straight to the sun. The original meaning of 是 is non-skew or straight. In modern Chinese it is used as a copula to express judgment.

问　上三包围结构 shàng sān bāowéi jiégòu　Left-top-right surrounding structure　门　口

It's ancient writing is 䦛. The ancient writing of 门（mén）is 䦔 which looks like a door. The ancient writing of 口（kǒu）is 㠯 which means mouth. 问 means knock on the door and ask sb about sth.

📋 注释 Notes

怎样问姓名　How to ask the name

一般情况下，如果对方和你同龄或者比你年龄小，可以用："请问，你叫什么名字？"如果对方比你年长，可以用："请问，您叫什么？"这样的问话，显得更加尊重；然后，为显诚意，可以先报上自己的名字，问的时候要不卑不亢，落落大方，可以用"您好，我叫×××，请问您怎么称呼？"

In general, if the other party is the same age as you or younger than you, you can use "Excuse me, what is your（你）name？" to ask; if the other party is older than you, you can use "Excuse me, what is your（您）name？" This will be more respectful to the other party; then, in order to show your sincerity, you can first state your name. When asking, you should not be humble or overbearing, but be generous. You can use "Hello, my name is ×××; may I know your name？"

中国人的姓名文化以及见面问姓名的礼仪　Chinese name culture and the etiquette of meeting and asking names

中国约有 20000 个姓，大部分都有几千年的历史了，如张、王、李、刘等。有的姓只有一个字，如张、王、赵、李，叫做单姓；有的姓有两个或两个以上的汉字，如：欧阳、司马、上官等，叫做复姓。中国人通过姓，可以追溯他的祖先。例如张姓，是中国第三大姓，出自轩辕黄帝（前 2717—前 2599 年）的儿子挥。因为他发明了弓箭，于是便被赐姓张。"张"的古文字形就是张弓射箭的样子。

There are more than 20,000 Chinese surnames, most of which have a history of thousands of years, such as Wang, Li, Zhang, and Liu. Some surnames have only one character and are called single surnames, such as Zhang, Wang, Zhao, and Li. Some surnames have two or more Chinese characters and are called compound surnames, such as Ouyang, Sima, Shangguan, and Ximen. By surname, ancestors can be traced. The surname Zhang, the third largest surname in China, comes from the Yellow Emperor, Xuan Yuan (2717 BC—2599 BC). His son wielded the bow and arrow, so he was given the surname Zhang. The ancient Chinese Character of "张" looks like an archery. There are more and more people who are good at inventing machinery, caring for their people, and relying on him, and the Zhang family has gradually prospered.

语法 Grammar

疑问代词"什么"　Interrogative pronoun "什么"

疑问代词"什么"表示疑问，用在疑问句中可直接做宾语，或者与后接名词性成分一起做宾语。

The interrogative pronoun "什么" expresses a question, and can be used as an object directly in an interrogative sentence, or as an object with a noun component followed by it.

主语 + 谓语 + 什么(Subject + Predicate + 什么)

主语 + 谓词 + 什么 + 名字(Subject + Predicate + 什么 + 名字)

A：你叫什么?

B：我叫一明。

A：您叫什么名字?

B：我叫大江。

用"吗"的疑问句　Interrogative sentences with "吗"

疑问助词"吗"表示疑问语气，加在陈述句句尾构成疑问句。如：

The interrogative particle "吗" represents the interrogative mood and is added at the end of the declarative sentence to form an interrogative sentence, e.g:

你叫大山吗?

他叫一明吗?

人称代词 Personal pronoun

人称代词	单 数	复 数
第一人称 first person	我 I/me	我们 we/us
第二人称 second person	你 you	你们 you
第三人称 third person	他 he/him	他们 they/them
	她 she/her	她们 they/them

练习 Exercises

一、听后选择正确的读音 Listen and choose the correct pronunciation

1. ( ) 您好 A. nín hǎo   B. nīn hǎo   C. níng hǎo

2. ( ) 什么 A. shéngme   B. shénme   C. shénmè

3. ( ) 请问 A. qǐnwèn   B. qǐngwèng   C. qǐngwèn

4. ( ) 谢谢 A. xièxie   B. xièxiè   C. xièxié

5. ( ) 你们 A. nínmen   B. nǐmén   C. nǐmen

6. ( ) 欢迎 A. huānyíng   B. huānyín   C. huānyǐng

二、听后给词语选择正确图片 Listen and choose the right picture

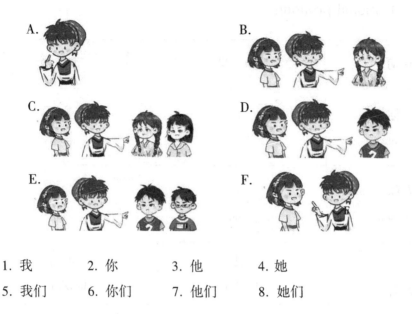

A.　　　　　　　　　B.

C.　　　　　　　　　D.

E.　　　　　　　　　F.

　　1. 我　　　　2. 你　　　　3. 他　　　　4. 她

　　5. 我们　　　6. 你们　　　7. 他们　　　8. 她们

三、请用下列词语填空 Please fill in the blanks with the following words

　　A. 你们　　　B. 叫　　　C. 你好　　　D. 称呼　　　E. 谢谢

　　例如：我（ B ）大山。

　　1. （　　　　　），你叫一明吗？

　　2. 您好，您怎么（　　　　　）？

　　3. A：欢迎（　　　　　）！

　　　　B：（　　　　　）！

四、汉字练习 Chinese character practice

　　1. 找出与现代汉字对应的古代汉字 Match the ancient Chinese characters and the modern Chinese characters

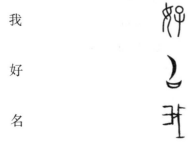

　　　　我

　　　　好

　　　　名

2. 分析下列汉字的结构 Analyze the structure of the following Chinese characters

我　你　问　的　好　欢　是　名

左右结构 Left-right structure _____

上下结构 Upper-lower structure _____

包围结构 Three-sided surrounding structure _____

独体字 Single character _____

3. 写出下列汉字的笔画。Write the strokes of the following Chinese characters

我 _____

你 _____

她 _____

他 _____

您 _____

五、书写练习 Writing exercises

1. 书写汉字 Writing Chinese characters

例如：我 jiào（叫）小米。

（1）你 hǎo（　　　　），我叫一明。

（2）欢 yíng（　　　　）你们。

（3）谢 xie（　　　　）！

2. 按正确的顺序组合句子并书写在横线上 Assemble the sentences in the correct order and write them on the line

例如：叫　我　大山。

　　　我叫大山。

（1）名字　什么　叫　你

_____

（2）请问　叫　吗　你　一明

_____

（3）您　称呼　怎么　请问

_____

六、课堂活动 Class activities

参照课文互相询问姓名。

Ask each other's names according to the text.

第二课　你是哪国人？
Lesson 2　Which country are you from?

📅 课文 Text

课文一　Text 1

从机场出来，一明、大江、大山、小米乘地铁回学校的路上，四人并排坐在一起。

After getting out of the airport, Yi Ming, Da Jiang, Da Shan and Xiao Mi take the subway back to school and they sit side by side.

（大江和小米挨着坐一起。）

(Da Jiang sits next to Xiao Mi.)

小米：你是哪国人？

大江：我是美国人。你是法国人吗？

小米：不是，我不是法国人。我是英国人。

课文二　Text 2

（一明和大山挨着坐一起。）

(Yi Ming sits next to Da Shan.)

一明：你是哪国人？

大山：我是法国人。

一明：小米是美国人吗？

大山：不是，她不是美国人，她是英国人。

课文三　Text 3

大江是美国人。大山是法国人。小米是英国人，不是法国人。

生词 New Words

生　词	词　性	解　释	举　例
哪 nǎ	adv	where	办公室在哪? Where is the office?
国 guó	n	country	世界上有许多国家。 There are lots of countries in the world.
人 rén	n	person; people	你是哪国人? Which country are you from?
美国 Měiguó	n	United States of America (USA)	美国是一个大国。 The USA is a big country.
美国人 Měiguó rén	n	American	亚伯拉罕·林肯是美国人。 Abraham Lincoln is an American.
法国 Fǎguó	n	France	法国在欧洲。 France is located in Europe.
法国人 Fǎguó rén	n	French	维克多·雨果是法国人。 Victor Hugo is a French.
英国 Yīngguó	n	United Kingdom(UK); Britain; England	英国是一个美丽的国家。 The UK is a beautiful country.
英国人 Yīngguó rén	n	the British/English	威廉·莎士比亚是英国人。 William Shakespeare is a British.
不 bù	adv	not; no	我不是一名警察。 I am not a policeman.
不是 bú shì		be not	你是美国人吗? Are You American? 不, 我不是美国人。 No, I'm not American.

汉 汉字 Chinese Characters

独体字(dútǐzì) Single character

人

The ancient writing of 人 is ↑ like the profile of a standing man.

不

美

The ancient writing of 美 is 羍. It looks like a person wearing a horn or feather ornament on the head. Its primitive sense is beautiful.

合体字(hétǐzì) Combined character

哪 左右结构 zuǒyòu jiégòu Left-right structure 口 那

The left part 口(kǒu) is mouth which means ask sb about sth. The right part is 那(nà) which means there, and its pronunciation is similar to 哪. Therefore 哪 is a signific-phonetic character.

法 左右结构 zuǒyòu jiégòu Left-right structure 氵 去

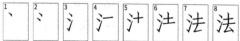

Its original meaning is law;. The left part 氵 is 水(shuǐ) water, which means the law is fair and just like water. The right part is 去(qù) and tis ancient writing is like a person walking. 法 is an associative character which means people have to follow the rules or will be punished.

国 四包围结构 sì bāo wéi jié gòu Complete surrounding structure 囗 玉

国 is composed of 囗(wéi) which means territory and 玉(yù) jade stands for power. 国 is an ideograph character means country.

英 上下结构 shàngxià jié gòu Upper-lower structure 艹 央

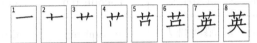

Its original meaning is flower. The upper part 艹(草, cǎo) means grass. The lower part 央(yāng) means center, and its pronunciation is similar to 英 (yīng). 英 is a signific-phonetic character.

📋 注释 Notes

国家、人、语言 Country、Person、Language

汉字	汉语拼音	英文	汉字	汉语拼音	英文
中国	Zhōngguó	China	中国人	Zhōngguó rén	Chinese
日本	Rìběn	Japan	日本人	Rìběn rén	Japanese
美国	Měiguó	America	美国人	Měiguó rén	American
英国	Yīngguó	England	英国人	Yīngguó rén	British
意大利	Yìdàlì	Italy	意大利人	Yìdàlì rén	Italian
印度	Yìndù	India	印度人	Yìndù rén	Indian

续表

汉字	汉语拼音	英文	汉字	汉语拼音	英文
澳大利亚	Àodàlìyà	Australia	澳大利亚人	Àodàlìyà rén	Australian
韩国	Hánguó	Korea	韩国人	Hánguó rén	Korean
西班牙	Xībānyá	Spain	西班牙人	Xībānyá rén	Spanish
泰国	Tàiguó	Thailand	泰国人	Tàiguó rén	Thai
德国	Déguó	Germany	德国人	Déguó rén	German
巴西	Bāxī	Brazil	巴西人	Bāxī rén	Brazilian
法国	Fǎguó	France	法国人	Fǎguó rén	French
越南	Yuènán	Vietnam	越南人	Yuènán rén	Vietnamese
墨西哥	Mòxīgē	Mexico	墨西哥人	Mòxīgē rén	Mexican
俄罗斯	Éluósī	Russia	俄罗斯人	Éluósī rén	Russian

语法 Grammar

疑问代词"哪"　Interrogative pronoun "哪"

疑问代词"哪"用在疑问句中，可以表示要求在几个人或者事物中确定一个，其结构形式：

The interrogative pronoun "哪" is used in interrogative sentences to indicate that one of several people or things is required to be identified. Its structural form is：

哪+名词+名词？　　哪+Noun+Noun？

例如：

A：你是哪国人？

B：我是美国人。

A：老师是哪国人？

B：老师是中国人。

"是"字句 "be" sentence structure

"是"字句是由"是"构成的判断句，用于表达人或事物等于什么或者属于什么。

"是" sentence is a judgment sentence composed of "is", which is used to express what a person or thing is equal to or belongs to.

语序：主语 + 谓语 + 宾语

Word order：Subject+ Predicate +Object

我是美国人。

她是法国人。

他是英国人。

其否定形式是在"是"前加上否定副词"不"。例如：

Its negative form is to add the negative adverb "不" before "是", e.g.

我不是美国人。

她不是法国人。

他不是英国人。

练习 Exercises

一、请听下面的词语选择对应的拼音 Please listen to the following words and choose the corresponding pinyin

1. (　　) A. bú shì　　　　B. bù hǎo　　　　C. bú tòng

2. (　　) A. guójiā　　　　B. guójí　　　　C. guójiè

3. (　　) A. shēngyīn　　　B. yǔyán　　　　C. wénzì

4. (　　) A. āyī　　　　　B. āyí　　　　　C. āyì

5. (　　) A. nín hǎo　　　　B. nín hāo　　　　C. nín hào

二、选择所给词语的正确读音 Choose the correct pronunciation of the words given

1. (　　) 哪　　　　A. nǎ　　　　B. lǎ　　　　C. nà

2. (　　) 不是　　　A. bù shì　　　B. bú shì　　　C. bú shi

3. (　　) 英国　　　A. Yīngguó　　B. Yīnguó　　C. Yīngguó

4. (　　) 法国　　　A. Fàguó　　　B. Fǎguó　　　C. Fǎguo

5. (　　)美国人　　　A. Měiguó rén　　　B. Měiguó réng　　　C. Měiguo rén

三、请用下列词语填空 Please fill in the blanks with the following words

A. 哪　　　B. 是　　　C. 人　　　D. 吗　　　E. 不是

例如：我（B）美国人。

1. 你是(　　　　)国人？

2. 大山是法国(　　　　)。

3. A：你是英国人(　　　　)？

　　B：(　　　　)，我不是英国人，我是法国人。

四、汉字练习 Chinese character practice

1. 找出现代汉字对应的古代汉字 Match the ancient Chinese characters and the modern Chinese characters

人

美

法

2. 分析下列汉字的结构 Analyze the structure of the following Chinese characters

人　　不　　美　　哪　　法　　国　　英

左右结构 Left-right structure _____

上下结构 Upper-lower structure _____

四包围结构 Complete surrounding structure _____

独体字 Single character _____

3. 写出下列汉字的笔画 Write the strokes of the following Chinese characters

美 _____

哪 _____

法 _____

国 _____

英 _____

五、书写练习 Writing exercises

1. 书写汉字 Writing Chinese characters

例如：我 shì(是)英国人。

(1)你是 nǎ(   )国人。

(2)我是 měi(   )国人。

(3)我 bú(   )是法国人。

2. 按正确的顺序组合句子并书写在横线上 Assemble the sentences in the correct order and write them on the line

例如：是　　我　　法国　　人

　　　我是法国人。

(1)吗　　你　　是　　英国　　人

_____

(2)他　　哪　　是　　人　　国

_____

(3)不是　　我　　美国　　人

_____

六、课堂活动 Class activities

两人一组，互相询问国籍。

In pairs, ask each other about their nationalities.

第三课　你今年多大？
Lesson 3　How old are you?

📅 课文 Text

课文一　Text 1

从机场出来，四人乘地铁回学校的路上。一明、大江、大山、小米四人并排坐在一起，继续聊天。

After coming out of the airport, four people are on their way back to school by subway. Yi Ming, Da Jiang, Da Shan and Xiao Mi sit side by side and continue to chat.

（大江和小米挨着坐一起。）

(Da Jiang and Xiao Mi sit next to each other.)

小米：你今年多大？

大江：我今年 23 岁。你今年多大？

小米：我今年 20 岁。

课文二　Text 2

（一明和大山挨着坐一起。）

(Yi Ming and Da Shan sit next to each other.)

一明：你今年多大？

大山：我今年 21 岁。你今年多大？

一明：我今年 24 岁。

（大山从包里取记事本时，从记事本里掉出一张照片。）

(When Da Shan took a notepad from his bag, a photo fell out of the notepad.)

一明：这是什么？

大山：这是我家人的照片。

一明：(指着其中一个小孩子 Pointing to one of the children)这孩子是谁呀？

大山：是我女儿。

一明：您女儿今年几岁了？

大山：一岁。

一明：(又指着其中一个人 And pointing to the other)这位是谁呀？

大山：是我妈妈。

一明：您妈妈多大年纪了？

大山：52 岁。

课文三 Text 3

小米今年 20 岁，大山今年 21 岁，大江今年 23 岁，一明今年 24 岁。

大山的妈妈 52 岁。

📝 生词 New Words

生　词	词　性	解　释	举　例
今年 jīnnián	n	this year	今年我计划去旅游。 I plan to travel this year.
多 duō	adv	used in questions how	食堂有多远？ How far is the canteen?
大 dà	adj	(of age) old	年龄(age)多大？ How old?
岁 suì	n	year	他今年二十岁。 He is twenty years old.
这 zhè	pronoun	this	这是大山的衣服吗？ Is this Da Shan's clothes?
个 gè	quant	used to modify a noun without a special quantifier	这个人 this person 这个国家 this country

续表

生 词	词 性	解 释	举 例
妈妈 māma	n	mom	我的妈妈是一名医生. My mom is a doctor.
家人 jiārén	n	family	我的家人也在中国。 My family is in China as well.
照片 zhàopiàn	n	picture；photo	家人的照片 family photos
这位 zhèwèi		this person（used to refer to a person to show respect，it is the honorific form of 这个人）	这位是我的老师。 This is my teacher.
谁 shuí	pronoun	who；whom	这位是谁？ Who's this？
呀 ya	interjection	wow（used instead of 啊 after a syllable ending in a，e，i，o，or ü）	这是谁呀？ Who's this？
年纪 niánjì	n	age；years	多大年纪？How old？
几 jǐ	numeral	used to ask about quantity and time	几个？ How many？ 几点？ What time？
几岁 jǐ suì		how old	你几岁了？ How old are you？
女儿 nǚér	n	daughter	你女儿几岁？ How old is your daughter？

汉 汉字 Chinese Characters

独体字(dútǐzì) Single character

女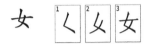

The ancient writing of 女 is 𗧶. It looks like an ancient woman kneeling and crossing her hands in front of body.

合体字(hétǐzì) Combined character

妈 左右结构 zuǒyòu jiégòu Left-right structure 女 马

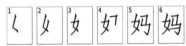

It is a signific-phonetic character. The signific element is 女 which represents female, the phonetic element is 马 mǎ which represents the pronounciation but the tone is different. 妈 is a high-level tone and 马 is a falling-rising tone.

位 左右结构 zuǒyòu jiégòu Left-right structure 亻 立

谁 左右结构 zuǒyòu jiégòu Left-right structure 讠 隹

It is a signific-phonetic character. The signific element is 讠 which represents language, the phonetic element is 隹(zhuī) which represents the similar sound.

纪 左右结构 zuǒyòu jiégòu Left-right structure 纟 己

It is a significic-phonetic character. The significic element is 纟 which represents silk thread (for sewing); silk yarn, the phonetic element is 几(jǐ) which represents the similar sound. Its primitive sense is to put in order silks.

多 上下结构 shàngxià jiégòu   Upper-lower structure

It is an ideograph. It is composed of two 夕 to express many.

岁 上下结构 shàngxià jiégòu   Upper-lower structure

It is an ideograph character. It is composed of two elements：山(shān, mountain) and 夕(xī, night). 岁 means year.

照 上下结构 shàngxià jiégòu   Upper-lower structure

It is a significic-phonetic character. The significic element is 灬 which represents fire, the phonetic element is 昭(zhào) which represents the same sound.

年 上下结构 shàngxià jiégòu   Upper-lower structure

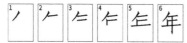

It is an ideograph. Its ancient writing is ⚘ , the upper element is 禾(hé) represents mature seedlings, the lower element represents 人. The character looks like a man carrying mature seedlings to express a year's harvest.

注释 Notes

时间词"年" Time word "所"

汉 语	拼 音	英 文
前年	qiánnián	the year before last year
去年	qùnián	last year
今年	jīnnián	this year
明年	míngnián	next year
后年	hòunián	the year after next year
每年	měinián	every year

亲属称谓 Relative title

汉 语	拼 音	英 文
爷爷	yéye	grandpa
奶奶	nǎinai	grandma
爸爸	bàba	father
妈妈	māma	mather
儿子	érzi	son
女儿	nǚér	daughter
哥哥	gēge	elder brother
弟弟	dìdi	younger brother
姐姐	jiějie	elder sister
妹妹	mèimei	younger sister
舅舅	jiùjiu	uncle
姑姑	gūgu	aunt

20 以下数字　Numbers below 20

阿拉伯数字	中文小写数字	拼音	英文	阿拉伯数字	中文小写数字	拼音	英文
0	〇	líng	zero	11	十一	shíyī	eleven
1	一	yī	one	12	十二	shíèr	twelve
2	二	èr	two	13	十三	shísān	thirteen
3	三	sān	three	14	十四	shísì	fourteen
4	四	sì	four	15	十五	shíwǔ	fifteen
5	五	wǔ	five	16	十六	shíliù	sixteen
6	六	liù	six	17	十七	shíqī	seventeen
7	七	qī	seven	18	十八	shíbā	eighteen
8	八	bā	eight	19	十九	shíjiǔ	nineteen
9	九	jiǔ	nine	20	二十	èrshí	twenty
10	十	shí	ten				
0.1	零点一	língdiǎnyī	zero point one	2/3	三分之二	sānfēnzhīèr	two-thirds

🗨 语法 Grammar

疑问代词"谁"　The interrogative pronoun "谁"

疑问代词"谁"在疑问句中用来询问人。"谁"可以用在主语的位置，也可以用在宾语的位置。

The interrogative pronoun "谁" is used to ask people in interrogative sentences. "谁" can be used in the position of the subject or the position of the object.

谁 + Verb + Object + ？

例如：A：谁是一明？

B：我是一明。

A：谁是中国人？

B：我是中国人。

Subject + Verb + 谁 + ?

例如：A：这位是谁？

B：她是我妈妈。

A：这孩子是谁？

B：她是我女儿。

疑问代词"几" The interrogative pronoun "几"

疑问代词"几"用来询问数量的多少，一般用于询问 10 以下的数字。"几"后边一般要加上相应的量词来提问。

The interrogative pronoun "几" is used to inquire about the quantity, and is generally used to inquire about numbers below 10. The corresponding quantifier is usually added after "几" to ask questions.

几 + 量词 + ?

例如：A：她几岁？

B：她四岁

A：你女儿几岁？

B：我女儿三岁。

"多+大"表示疑问 "多+大" means doubt

"多+大"表示疑问，用于询问年龄。例如：

"多 + 大" indicates a question and is used to ask about age, e.g.

例如：小米：你今年多大？

大江：我今年 23 岁。

一明：您妈妈多大年纪了？

大山：52 岁了。

结构助词"的" Structural particle "的"

名词或代词带"的"修饰名词，表示领属关系。

When a noun or a pronoun followed by "的" modifies a noun, it indicates a possessive relationship.

名词1 + 的 + 名词2

Noun1 + 的 + Noun2

中国　的　书

大山　的　书

小米　的　书

人称代词 + 的 + 名词2

Pronoun +　的 + Noun2

我　　的　　书

你　　的　　书

他　　的　　书

当"的"后边的名词是亲属称谓或者指人的名词时，"的"可以省略。例如：

When the nouns behind "的" are kinship terms or nouns referring to people, "的" can be omitted，e.g.

我(的)妈妈　　我(的)爸爸　　我(的)朋友

练习 Exercises

一、听后选择正确的读音 Listen and choose the correct pronunciation

1. (　　) A. duō 　　　B. shǎo 　　　C. lǎo

2. (　　) A. líng 　　　B. wǔ 　　　C. shí

3. (　　) A. yéye 　　　B. bàba 　　　C. gēge

4. (　　) A. māma 　　　B. jiějie 　　　C. dìdi

5. (　　) A. jīnnián 　　　B. qiánnián 　　　C. měinián

二、选择所给词语的正确读音 Choose the correct pronunciation of the words given

1. (　　) 零　　　A. líng 　　　B. lín 　　　C. līng

2. (　　) 三　　　A. sāng 　　　B. sān 　　　C. sǎn

3. (　　) 年纪　　A. niánjì 　　　B. niánjí 　　　C. niànjí

4. (　　) 今年　　A. jīngnián 　　　B. jīnnián 　　　C. jīnniǎn

5. (　　) 明年　　A. míngniǎn 　　　B. mínnián 　　　C. míngnián

三、请用下列词语填空 Please fill in the blanks with the following words

A. 今年　　B. 是　　C. 女儿　　D. 年纪　　E. 岁　　F. 谁的　　G. 的

例如：你(A)多大了？

1. 我今年24(　　　　)。

2. A：她(　　　　)我妈妈。

　　B：您妈妈多大(　　　　)了？

3. A：这是(　　　　)的孩子？

　　B：这是我(　　　　)孩子。

4. 她是我的(　　　　)。

四、汉字练习 Chinese character practice

1. 找出现代汉字对应的古代汉字

Match the ancient Chinese characters and the modern Chinese characters

年

女

多

2. 分析下列汉字的结构 Analyze the structure of the following Chinese characters

岁　位　照　谁　多

上下结构 Upper-lower structure _____

左右结构 Left-right structure _____

3. 写出下列汉字的笔画 Write the strokes of the following Chinese characters

儿_____

个_____

女_____

年_____

家_____

五、书写练习 Writing exercises

1. 按正确的顺序组合句子并书写在横线上 Assemble the sentences in the correct order and write them on the line

例如：大　多　你　今年

　　　你今年多大？

（1）呀　这位　谁　是

_____

（2）是　他　爸爸　我

_____

（3）您　几　岁　女儿　今年　了

_____

（4）家人　是　这　照片　的　我

_____

（5）妈妈　了　您　年纪　多大

_____

2. 书写汉字 Writing Chinese characters

例如：我 jīnnián（今年）23 岁了。

（1）您妈妈多大 niánjì（　　　　　）了？

（2）这是我 nǚér（　　　　　）。

（3）这位是 shéi（　　　　　）？

（4）他是我 bàba（　　　　　）。

（5）她是我的 jiārén（　　　　　）。

六、课堂活动 Class activities

两个人一组，互相询问年龄。

In groups of two, ask each other about their age.

第四课 你学什么专业？
Lesson 4　What's your major?

📅 课文 Text

课文一　Text 1

从地铁口出来，去学校的路上。

Coming out of the subway exit, on the way to the school.

（大江替小米提着行李，和小米边走边聊天。）

（Da Jiang is carrying luggage for Xiao Mi and chatting with Xiao Mi while walking.）

小米：你是什么专业？

大江：我是计算机专业。你呢？

小米：我也是计算机专业，我们都是计算机专业。

课文二　Text 2

（一明替大山提着行李，和大山边走边聊天。）

（Yi Ming is carrying luggage for Da Shan and chatting with Da Shan while walking.）

一明：你是什么专业？

大山：我是建筑专业，你呢？

一明：我是交通专业。

大山：我们专业不同。

一明：是的。

课文三　Text 3

小米是计算机专业，大江也是计算机专业，他们都是计算机专业。

大山是建筑专业，一明是交通专业，他们的专业不同。

生词 New Words

生　词	词　性	解　释	举　例
专业 zhuānyè	n	special field of study	什么专业？ What's your major?
计算机 jìsuànjī	n	computer	计算机可以解决复杂的问题。 Computers can solve hard questions.
计算机专业 jìsuànjī zhuānyè	n	computer science major	我主修计算机专业。 I major in computer science.
呢 ne	part	a modal particle used at the end of a declarative sentence to indicate the continuation of an action or a situation	一明现在正在图书馆呢。 Yi ming is in the library now.
我们 wǒmen	pronoun	we; us	我们是同班同学。 We are classmates.
也 yě	adv	also; too; as well; either	我也是计算机专业。 My major is also computer science.
都 dōu	adv	all; both	我们都是计算机专业。 We are all computer professionals.
建筑 jiànzhù	n	building; structure; edifice	我们学校里有许多老建筑。 There are many old buildings in our school.

续表

生　词	词　性	解　释	举　例
建筑专业 jiànzhù zhuānyè	n	architecture major	小米主修建筑专业。 Xiao Mi majors in architecture.
交通专业 jiāotōng zhuānyè	n	transportation major	大山主修交通专业。 Da Shan majors in transportation.
同 tóng	adj	similar；same	我们来自同一个国家。 We are from the same country.
相同 xiāngtóng	adj	identical；the same；alike	这两个词具有相同的意思。 The meaning of these two words are the same.
不同 bùtóng	adj	not alike；different	不同专业 different majors
他们 tāmen	pron	they；them	他们不是我们学校的学生。 They are not the students of our school.

汉 汉字 Chinese Characters

独体字(dútǐzì)　**Single character**

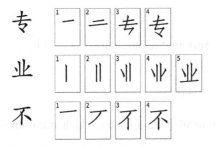

合体字(hétǐzì)　Combined character

计　左右结构 zuǒyòu jiégòu　Left-right structure　讠 十

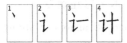

It is an ideograph. It is composed of 讠(yán, languge) and 十(shí, number ten) to express to count.

机　左右结构 zuǒyòu jiégòu　Left-right structure　木 几

It is a signific-phonetic character. The signific element is 木 which represents wood, the phonetic element is 几(jī; jǐ) which represents the sound.

都　左右结构 zuǒyòu jiégòu　Left-right structure　者 阝

他　左右结构 zuǒyòu jiégòu　Left-right structure　亻 也

建　左下包围结构 zuǒxià bāowéi jiégòu　Lower-left Surrounding structure　廴 聿

通　左下包围结构 zuǒxià bāowéi jiégòu　Lower-left Surrounding structure　辶 甬

It is a signific-phonetic character. The signific element is 辶 (chuò) which represents walking, the phonetic element is 甬 (yǒng) which represents the similar sound. The primitive of sense of 通 is to arrive.

同 上三包围结构 shàng sān bāowéi jiégòu Left-top-right surrounding structure 冂 冋(一 口)

| 1 丨 | 2 冂 | 3 冂 | 4 冋 | 5 同 | 6 同 |

It is an ideograph. The ancient writing is 同, the upper part 同 represents the heavy loads people carry together. The lower part 同(口, mouth）represents slogans people shout when they work together. The primitive of sense of 同 is to unite in a concerted effort. Its extended sense refers to 相同（same）.

算 上下结构 shàngxià jiégòu Upper-lower structure 𥫗 鼻(目 廾)

| 1 丿 | 2 ⺊ | 3 𠂉 | 4 𥫗 | 5 𥫗 | 6 𥫗 | 7 竹 | 8 笮 | 9 筲 | 10 笪 | 11 管 | 12 箟 | 13 算 | 14 算 |

筑 上下结构 shàngxià jiégòu Upper-lower structure 𥫗 巩（工 凡）

| 1 丿 | 2 ⺊ | 3 𠂉 | 4 𥫗 | 5 𥫗 | 6 𥫗 | 7 𥫗 | 8 竺 | 9 笁 | 10 筇 | 11 筑 | 12 筑 |

📋 注释 Notes

理工科专业称谓 Professional title of science and engineering

汉 语	拼 音	英 文
建筑学	jiànzhùxué	Architecture
计算机	jìsuànjī	Computer Science
数学	shùxué	Math
物理	wùlǐ	Physics
生物	shēngwù	Biology
医学	yīxué	Medicine

汉　语	拼　音	英　文
能源	néngyuán	Energy
自动化	zìdònghuà	Automation
信息工程	xìnxīgōngchéng	Information engineering
人工智能	réngōngzhìnéng	Artificial Intelligence

💬 语法 Grammar

疑问句"Noun+呢" "Noun+呢" Questions

在一定的上下文里，名词或代词后面加上"呢"可以构成省略式疑问句。例如：

In a certain context，"呢" can be added to a noun or a pronoun to form an elliptical question，e.g.

Noun + 呢？

A：你是哪国人？

B：我是英国人，你呢？

A：我是法国人。

A：你是什么专业？

B：我是交通专业，你呢？

A：我是计算机专业。

副词"也"和"都" The adverbs "也"and "都"

副词"也"和"都"一般放在动词或形容词前边，在句中作状语。例如：

The adverbs "也"and "都"are placed before vebs and adjectives and function as adverbials，e.g.

1. 他是中国人，我也是中国人，我们都是中国人。

2. 我今年 20 岁，他也 20 岁，我们都是 20 岁。

3. 我是计算机专业，他也是计算机专业，我们都是计算机专业。

练习 Exercises

一、请听下面的词语选择对应的拼音 Please listen to the following words and choose the corresponding pinyin

1. (　　) A. zhuānyè　　　　　B. jìnéng　　　　　　C. xìnxī

2. (　　) A. shùxué　　　　　　B. wùlǐ　　　　　　　C. shēngwù

3. (　　) A. jiànzhùxué　　　　B. jìsuànjī　　　　　　C. zìdònghuà

4. (　　) A. bútòng　　　　　　B. bùtóng　　　　　　C. bùtōng

5. (　　) A. jiāotōng　　　　　B. jiāotóng　　　　　　C. jiāotòng

二、选择所给词语的正确读音 Choose the correct pronunciation of the words given

1. (　　) 什么　　A. shéngme　　B. shénme　　　C. shénmè

2. (　　) 专业　　A. zhānyè　　　B. zhuānyè　　　C. zhuānye

3. (　　) 交通　　A. jiāotōng　　B. jiāntōng　　　C. jiàotōng

4. (　　) 建筑　　A. jiàngzhù　　B. jiànzhu　　　C. jiànzhù

5. (　　) 计算机　A. jìsuànjī　　B. jìsànjī　　　C. jìsuànjì

三、请用下列词语填空 Please fill in the blanks with the following words

A. 也　　B. 专业　　C. 建筑　　D. 不同　　E. 都　　F. 呢

例如：我们的专业（ D ）。

1. 我(　　　　　)是计算机专业。

2. 我们(　　　　　)是交通专业

3. A：你是什么(　　　　　)？

　　B：我是(　　　　　)专业。

4. A：我是法国人，你(　　　　　)？

　　B：我是美国人。

四、汉字练习 Chinese character practice

1. 写出下列古代汉字对应的现代汉字　Write the modern Chinese character of the following ancient Chinese character

2. 分析下列汉字的结构 Analyze the structure of the following Chinese characters

机　　通　　计　　建　　筑　　通　　他

左右结构 Left-right structure _____

上下结构 Upper-lower structure _____

左下包围结构 Lower-left surrounding structure _____

3. 写出下列汉字的笔画 Write the strokes of the following Chinese characters

专 _____

业 _____

我 _____

们 _____

筑 _____

建 _____

算 _____

五、书写练习 Writing exercises

1. 书写汉字 Writing Chinese characters

例如：你是什么 zhuānyè（专业）？

（1）我是 jiànzhù（　　　　）专业。

（2）我们 dōu（　　　　）是计算机专业。

（3）我 yě（　　　　）是交通专业

（4）我是 shùxué（　　　　）专业。

（5）我是医学专业，你 ne（　　　　）？

2. 按正确的顺序组合句子并书写在横线上 Assemble the sentences in the correct order and write them on the line

例如：什么　　专业　　你　　是

　　　你是什么专业？

（1）我　　计算机　　专业　　是

_____

(2) 是　　我们　　都　　交通　　专业

_____

(3) 不同　　的　　我们　　专业

_____

(4) 专业　　数学　　是　　我　　呢　　你

_____

(5) 专业　　我爸爸　　是　　也　　建筑

_____

六、课堂活动 Class activities

两人一组，互相询问专业。

Ask each other about their profession in pairs.

第五课　你为什么来中国留学？
Lesson 5　Why did you come to study in China?

📅 课文 Text

课文一　Text 1

（进入校门，四人继续聊着。大江替小米提着行李，和小米边走边聊天。）

（Entering the school gate, the four of them continue to chat. Da Jiang is carrying luggage for Xiao Mi and chatting with Xiao Mi while walking.）

小米：你为什么来中国留学？

大江：我喜欢中国文化。你呢？

小米：我也是因为喜欢中国文化，所以才来中国留学的。

课文二　Text 2

（一明替大山提着行李，和大山边走边聊天。）

（Yi Ming is carrying luggage for Da Shan and chatting with Da Shan while walking.）

一明：你为什么来中国留学？

大山：我喜欢中国建筑，想学习中国建筑，才来中国留学的。

一明：哦，明白了。

课文三　Text 3

小米因为喜欢中国的文化，才来中国留学的。

大山因为喜欢中国的建筑，想学习中国的建筑，才来中国留学的。

✍ 生词 New Words

生　词	词　性	解　释	举　例
为什么 wèi shénme	adv	why；for what reason	你为什么跑步这么快？ Why do you run so fast？
来 lái	vt	come	来看看我们的学校吧！ Come and see our school！
中国 Zhōngguó	n	China	欢迎来到中国。 Welcome to China.
文化 wénhuà	n	civilization；culture	每个国家的文化都是独特的。 The culture of every single country is unique.
中国文化 zhōngguó wénhuà	n	Chinese culture	我喜欢中国文化。 I like Chinese culture.
留学 liúxué	vt	study abroad/overseas	为什么来中国留学？ Why come to China to study abroad？
喜欢 xǐhuan	vt	like；love；be fond of；be keen on	我喜欢打篮球。 I love playing basketball.
因为 yīnwèi	conj	because；for；as；on account of	我喜欢北京，因为它很美。 I love Beijing because it is beautiful.
所以 suǒyǐ	conj	so；therefore；hence	明天有个考试，所以我今天 必须要学习。 There will be an exam tomorrow, so I must study today.
才 cái	adv	just	他刚刚才离开。 He has just left.
哦 ò	int	oh；ah	哦，我知道你的意思了。 Oh, I know what you mean.

续表

生 词	词 性	解 释	举 例
明白 míngbai	vt	know；realize；understand	我明白了单词的意思。 I understand the meaning of the word.
了 le	modal particle	used after the verb or adj to indicate to indicate that an action or change has been completed	我吃了。 I ate it.

汉 汉字 Chinese Characters

独体字(dútǐzì) Single character

为

The ancient writing is 𧰨, the upper part 𠂇 represents a hand. The lower part represents an elephant. The character describes a man is leading an elephant to do works. Its primitive sense is to do something. 为 is the modern Chinese simplified character.

中

The ancient writing is 𣃚, it looks like a flag with streamers to express the center of region.

上

Its oracle script is 二. The lower horizontal line looks like the horizon, the upper stroke looks like something on the horizon. Its primitive sense is upper.

文

The ancient writing is 文. It describes a standing man with a tattoo on the chest. Its primitive sense is tattoo. Its extended sense is characters and script.

才

白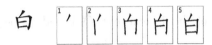

了 ㄱ 了

来

Its oracle script is 來. The pictographic script symbolizes the form of wheat. 来 (come) is its phonetic loaned sense.

合体字 (hétǐzì) Combined character

明 左右结构 zuǒyòu jiégòu Left-right structure 日 月

丨 冂 日 日 旫 明 明 明

The ancient writing is ◑. The ideograph is composed of two elements. The left part is ⊙ (日) which means the sun, the right element 𝒟 (月, yuè) which means the moon. It is an associative character which means bright.

留 上下结构 shàngxià jiégòu Upper-lower structure 丣 田

丶 匕 匕 刟 刟 𠃌 留 留 留 留

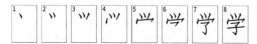

学　上下结构 shàngxià jiégòu　Upper-lower structure

The ancient writing is 𦥯, the ideograph is composed of four different pictographic elements: the upper element is 𦥑 , look like human's left and right hands, the middle part represents some small sticks for arithmetic. The element is a covering, and the element is a child or pupil. The ideographical structure expresses to teach children knowledge ( ) and let them get rid of the ignorance ( ) and to be enlightened.

语法 Grammar

语气助词"了"　The modal particle "了"

"了"用于句末，表示变化或新情况的出现。例如：

"了" is used at the end of a sentence to indicate the appearance of changes or new circumstances, e.g.

1. 我明白了。

2. 王老师的女儿今年 5 岁了。

3. 王老师去年 45 岁，今年 46 岁了。

关联词"因为……所以……"　The correlative "因为……所以……"

"因为……所以……"连接一个因果复句。表达事物的原因和结果。例如：

"因为……所以……" links a cause-effect complex sentence and explains the cause and effect of something, e.g.

1. 因为小米病了，所以没来上课。

2. 因为天气不好，所以没去打球。

3. 因为要去中国留学，所以学习汉语。

"因为"和"所以"都可以单独使用，"因为"表示原因；"所以"表示结果。例如：

Both "因为" and "所以" can be used separately. "因为" tells the cause, and "所以" tells the result, e.g.

1. 因为小米病了，没来上课。

2. 天气不好，所以没去打球。

📖 练习 Exercises

一、请听下面的词语选择对应的拼音 Please listen to the following words and choose the corresponding pinyin

1. (　　) A. lái　　　　　B. cái　　　　　C. ò

2. (　　) A. xiǎng　　　　B. guó　　　　　C. huà

3. (　　) A. wénhuà　　　B. liúxué　　　　C. xǐhuan

4. (　　) A. yīnwèi　　　 B. zhōngguó　　　C. wénhuà

5. (　　) A. wèishénme　 B. míngbaile　　　C. zhōngguózì

二、选择所给词语的正确读音 Choose the correct pronunciation of the words given

1. (　　) 来　　A. lái　　　　 B. lài　　　　　C. laí

2. (　　) 因为　A. yīnwei　　　B. yīngwèi　　　C. yīnwèi

3. (　　) 文化　A. wénhuà　　 B. wénhua　　　C. wénghuà

4. (　　) 留学　A. niúxué　　　B. liúxué　　　 C. liúxié

5. (　　) 明白　A. míngbai　　 B. mínbai　　　 C. mínbái

三、请用下列词语填空 Please fill in the blanks with the following words

A. 喜欢　　B. 为什么　　C. 学习　　D. 才　　E. 文化　　F. 了

例如：我(A)中国的建筑。

1. 小米因为喜欢中国的文化，(　　　　　)来中国留学的。

2. 我想(　　　　　)中国的建筑。

3. A：你(　　　　　)来中国留学？

　　B：我喜欢中国的(　　　　　)。

　　A：哦，明白(　　　　　)。

四、汉字练习 Chinese character practice

1. 找出现代汉字对应的古代汉字 Match the ancient Chinese characters and the modern Chinese characters

文

月

明

日

中

2. 分析下列汉字的结构 Analyze the structure of the following Chinese characters

留　　明　　学　　所　　因

上下结构 Upper-lower structure _____

左右结构 Left-right structure _____

全包围结构 Whole-surround structure _____

3. 写出下列汉字的笔画 Write the strokes of the following Chinese characters

中 _____

国 _____

文 _____

化 _____

明 _____

学 _____

五、书写练习 Writing exercises

1. 按正确的顺序组合句子并书写在横线上 Assemble the sentences in the correct order and write them on the line

例如：为什么　　留学　　你　　中国　　来

你为什么来中国留学?

(1)喜欢　　我　　文化　　中国

_____

(2)想　　建筑　　的　　中国　　学习　　我

_____

(3)美食　　中国　　的　　我　　喜欢

_____

(4)明白　　你　　我　　留学　　为什么　　吗

_____

(5)为什么　　美国　　去　　留学　　你

_____

2. 书写汉字 Writing Chinese characters

例如：我 xǐhuan（喜欢）中国的建筑。

(1)你为什么来中国 liúxué(　　　　)？

(2)我喜欢中国 wénhuà(　　　　)。

(3)míngbai(　　　　)了。

(4)我也喜欢 Zhōngguó(　　　　)的美食。

六、课堂活动 Class activities

两人一组，互相询问来中国留学的原因。

As a group of two, then asked each other why they came to study in China.

第六课　天气怎么样？

Lesson 6　What's the weather like?

📅 课文 Text

课文一　Text 1

在操场，一明、大江、大山和小米一起商量明天出去玩的事情。

On the playground, Yi Ming, Da Jiang, Da Shan and Xiao Mi discuss together about going out to play tomorrow.

（大山、一明来得较早。）

（Da Shan and Yi Ming come earlier.）

大山：小米呢？

一明：小米在家呢。

大山：你看天气预报了吗？

一明：没看，你看了吗？

大山：昨天看了。

一明：今天天气怎么样？

大山：天气预报说，天气不太好，是阴天，有风，但是风不太大。

一明：没有雨吗？

大山：没有。

一明：下午是晴天吗？

大山：是的

一明：没关系，可以去玩儿。

课文二 Text 2

（大江和小米从远处走来。）

（Da Jiang and Xiao Mi come from a distance.）

大江：明天我们去公园玩儿吗?。

大山：是的。但是天气预报说，明天是阴天，有风。

大江：没关系的，可以出去玩。

课文三 Text 3

明天星期六，阴天，有风。虽然天气不太好，但是他们还是出去玩。

生词 New Words

举 例	生 词	词 性		解 释
看 kàn	v	Watch; look; see		明天我要去看电影。 I will watch a movie tomorrow.
天气 tiānqì	n	weather		今天天气怎么样? What is the weather like today?
预报 yùbào	n	forecast		天气预报说今天有雨。 It is forecasted that today is a rainy day.
天气预报 tiānqì yùbào	n	weather forecast		看天气预报 watch the weather forecast
吗 ma	modal particle	used at the end of a sentence to express doubt		你看天气预报了吗? Have you seen the weather forecast?
没 méi	adv	not		我的工作还没完成。 My work has not been finished yet.
没有 méiyǒu	adv	not		他没有被邀请。 He is not invited.

举　例	生　词	词　性		解　释
说 shuō	vt	say		他没看。 He didn't watch.
太 tài	adv	excessively；too；over		声音太大了。 The voice is too loud.
阴天 yīntiān	n	overcast sky；cloudy day		明天是个阴天。 Tomorrow will be a cloudy day.
晴天 qíngtiān	n	fine/clear/sunny day		今天是个晴天。 Today is a sunny day.
风 fēng	n	wind		外面风很大。 The wind blows strong outside.
雨 yǔ	n	rain		今天不会有雨。 There will be no rain today.
上午 shàngwǔ	n	morning；forenoon		今天上午我去爬山了。 I went mountain climbing this morning.
下午 xiàwǔ	n	afternoon； post meridiem（pm）		明天下午有一个会议。 There will be a meeting tomorrow afternoon.
没关系 méi guānxi		it doesn't matter；that's all right；never mind		我为我的无礼道歉。没关系。 I apologize for my rudeness. Never mind.
虽然 suīrán	conj	though；although		虽然今天很冷，但我还是想去踢足球。 Although it is cold today, I still want to play soccer.
但是 dànshì	conj	but；yet；however；still		我们来自同一个国家，但是不是同一个城市。 We are from the same country but different cities.

续表

举 例	生 词	词 性		解 释
还是 háishi	adv	still; all the same		他还是没完成任务。 He still fails to complete the mission.

汉字 Chinese Characters

独体字(dútǐzì) Single character

The ancient writings are 𝍊、𝍊, and they depict raindrops falling from the sky. Its primitive sense is rain.

Its oracle script is ⌢. The upper horizontal line looks like the horizon, the lower stroke looks like something under the horizon. Its primitive sense is lower.

合体字(hétǐzì)　Combined character

阴　左右结构 zuǒyòu jiégòu　Left-right structure　阝　月

The ancient writing is 陰. It is a significant-phonetic character. The left

part 阝(阝) is the significant element. It represents 阜(fù, earth hummock). The right

part 侌 is the phonetic element. It represents the similar sound of the whole character.

The primitive sense of 陰 is the north of the mountain. It is the shady face. Its extended

sense is dark.

没　左右结构 zuǒyòu jiégòu　Left-right structure　氵　殳

The ancient writing is 沒 It is an ideographical structure. The left element is 氵(水 shuǐ,

water). The element 回 looks like something sank into the water. The element 又(又)

expresses to get the thing with your hand. The character describes things sink into the

water and cannot be reached by hand. Its primitive sense is to sink.

说　左右结构 zuǒyòu jiégòu　Left-right structure　讠　兑

It is an ideographical structure. The left element 讠 is the variation of

言(yán, to speak/talk/say). The right element 兑 is 悦(yuè, happy; pleased;

cheerful; joyful). It means to talk happily.

看　上下结构 shàngxià jiégòu　Upper-lower structure　手　目

The upper part is the variation of 手(shǒu, hand). The lower part is 目(mù, eyes).

The character looks like someone puts one hand above the eye to see far. It is an

ideographical structure.

🗨 语法 Grammar

动态助词"了"　The dynamic particle "了"

"了"表示动作或者状态的完成。例如：

"了" means the completion of an action or state, e.g.

吃了　　喝了　　睡了　　看了

读了　　听了　　买了　　卖了

动词"在"　The verb "在"

"在"表示存在，宾语一般为表示处所的词语。例如：

"在" can indicating existence, its object is usually a place, e.g.

A：你的家在哪儿?

B：我的家在北京。

否定式是在"在"的前面加"不"。例如：

The negative form is to place "bu" before "zɑi", e.g.

A：你的家不在上海吗?

B：我的家不在上海。

疑问代词"怎么样"　Interrogative pronoun "怎么样"

疑问代词"怎么样"用来询问状况，用于疑问句句尾。例如：

The interrogative pronoun "怎么样" is used to inquire about the situation and at the end of interrogative sentences, e.g.

一明：今天天气怎么样?

大山：天气不太好，是阴天，有风。

一明：明天天气怎么样?

大山：明天是晴天。

A：他怎么样?

B：他不太好。

关联词"虽然……但是……"   The correlative"虽然……但是……"

"虽然……但是……"连接两个分句，表示转折关系。先肯定和承认"虽然"后边的事实，然后突出"但是"后边的意思。例如：

"虽然……但是……"links two clauses and expresses a transition. This pattern first affirms and admits the fact following "虽然"，and then emphasizes the clause following"但是"，e.g.

1. 虽然明天阴天，但是可以出去玩儿。

2. 虽然天气很冷，但是教室里暖和。

3. 虽然学习的时间不长，但是说得很好。

"但是"可以单用。例如：

"但是"may be used independently，e.g.

4. 明天阴天，但是可以出去玩儿。

5. 天气很冷，但是教室里暖和。

6. 学习的时间不长，但是说得很好。

练习 Exercises

一、请听下面的词语选择对应的拼音 Listen and choose the correct pronunciation

1. (   )天气   A. tiānqì   B. tiānqī   C. yùbà

2. (   )下午   A. xiàwǔ   B. méiyǒu   C. tiānqì

3. (   )晴天   A. qíngtiān   B. yīntiān   C. suīrán

4. (   )预报   A. yúbǎo   B. yùbào   C. yùbǎo

5. (   )风   A. fèng   B. fēng   C. féng

二、听后选择正确的图片 Listen and choose the right picture

1. 阴天_____   2. 风_____   3. 晴天_____   4. 天气预报_____

5. 雨_____   6. 操场_____   7. 没关系_____   8. 下午_____

A.   B.   C.

D. ⬛ E. ☁ F. 🧑

三、选择所给词语的正确读音 Choose the correct pronunciation of the words given

1. ( ) 晴天　　A. qíntiān　　　　B. qíngtiān　　　　C. qīngtiān

2. ( ) 没有　　A. mèiyǒu　　　　B. méiyǒu　　　　　C. méiyóu

3. ( ) 天气　　A. tiānqì　　　　　B. tiānqī　　　　　　C. tiánqì

4. ( ) 但是　　A. dānshì　　　　　B. dànshì　　　　　　C. dànsì

5. ( ) 预报　　A. yùbào　　　　　B. yùbāo　　　　　　C. yǔbào

6. ( ) 可以　　A. kēyǐ　　　　　　B. kěyǐ　　　　　　　C. kēyī

四、汉字练习 Chinese character practice.

1. 找出现代汉字对应的古代汉字 Match the ancient Chinese characters and the modern Chinese characters

下　　　　　　𠕊

雨　　　　　　𣲙

没　　　　　　⌒

2. 分析下列汉字的结构 Analyze the structure of the following Chinese characters

然　但　晴　阴　是　虽　还

上下结构 Upper-lower structure _____

右上包围结构 Right-top surrounding structure _____

左下包围结构 Left-lower surrounding structure _____

3. 写出下列汉字的笔画 Write the strokes of the following Chinese characters

可 _____

以 _____

没 _____

有 _____

但 _____

是 _____

五、请用下列词语填空 Please fill in the blanks with the following words

A. 晴天　　B. 天气　　C. 雨　　D. 还是　　E. 没关系　　F. 下午　　G. 阴天

例如：今天下午有(C)，我们不能出去玩。

1. (　　　　　)，我们可以一起出去玩。

2. 今天(　　　　)真好，是(　　　　)。

3. 马上要下雨了，我们(　　　　)不出去了吧。

4. 我今天(　　　　)听汉语课。

5. 这里晴天很少，总是(　　　　)。

六、书写练习 Writing exercises

1. 按正确的顺序组合句子并书写在横线上 Assemble the sentences in the correct order and write them on the line

例如：叫　　我　　大山

　　　我叫大山。

(1)天气预报　　你　　看　　了　　吗

_____

(2)阴天　　今天　　是

_____

(3)明天　　下雨　　会　　吗

_____

(4)明天　　我　　玩儿　　出去

_____

(5)风　　说　　有　　天气预报　　下午

_____

2. 书写汉字 Writing Chinese characters

例如：我 jiào (叫)小米。

(1)我看了 tiān(　　　)气预报。

(2)今天晚上会下 yǔ(　　　)。

(3)明天是 qíng(　　　)天，我们可以一起出去玩。

(4)下午有 fēng(　　　)。

(5)你在 cāo chǎng(　　　)吗？

七、对话练习 Practice in conversation

1. 根据图片完成对话 Complete the conversation with the picture

一明：明天天气怎么样？

大山：天气预报说要下雨。

一明：那我们还是不要出去玩了。

大山：好。

2. 和同学设计一段谈论天气的对话 Design your conversation of talking about the weather with your partner

八、课堂活动 Class activities

完成下面表格，并和其他同学交流，说说他们在不同天气在哪里做什么。

Complete the table below and talk to other students about what they would like to do in different weathers.

例如：我下雨天在家看书。

谁（Who）	天气（Weather）	在哪里（Where）	做什么（What to do）
我	下雨天	在家	看书

第七课　现在几点？
Lesson 7　What time is it?

📅 课文 Text

课文一　Text 1

在教室，下课了，留学生大山和小米商量去食堂吃饭。

In the classroom, when class is over, international students Da Shan and Xiao Mi discuss going to the canteen to eat.

（大山背着包要走，小米喊住他。）

（Da Shan is about to leave with his bag on his back and Xiao Mi calls out to him.）

小米：大山，你去食堂吃饭吗？

大山：是的。你去吗？

小米：去，但是现在食堂的人太多了，我一会儿去。

大山：咱们一起去吧。

小米：好的。

课文二　Text 2

（两人一起看了一会儿书。）

（They read the book together for a while.）

大山：现在是几点？

小米：现在是 12 点半，食堂人应该少了，咱们走吧。

大山：好的。咱们去哪个食堂吃饭？

小米：去一食堂。

大山：去一食堂几楼？

小米：去一食堂 2 楼。

大山：好的。

课文三 Text 3

大山和小米 12 点半，一起去一食堂 2 楼吃饭。

📝 生词 New Words

生　词	词　性	解　释	举　例
食堂 shítáng	n	dining room；mess hall；canteen	从这走到食堂需要五分钟。 It takes 5 minutes to walk to the canteen from here.
一食堂 yī shítáng	n	dining room 1；mess hall 1；canteen1	我去食堂。 I go to the dining room.
吃 chī	vt	eat	我还没吃晚饭。 I haven't eaten dinner yet.
饭 fàn	n	meal	饭菜很好吃。 The meal tastes great.
吃饭 chī fàn		dine；have a meal	我去食堂吃饭。 I'm going to the canteen for a meal.
现在 xiànzài	adv	now；today；nowadays	现在八点了。 It is 8 o'clock now.
多 duō	adj	many；much；more	这里人很多。 There are many people here.

续表

生 词	词 性	解 释	举 例
少 shǎo	adj	few; little; less	今天学校人很少。 There are few people in the school today.
一会儿 yíhuìr	adv	a little while; in a minute	我一会儿就回来。 I will be back in a minute.
和 hé	conj	and	我在餐厅遇见了大山和小米。 I met Da Shan and Xiao Mi in the canteen.
点 diǎn	quant	o'clock; hour	明早十点有个会议。 There is a meeting at 10 o'clock tomorrow morning.
几点 jǐ diǎn		what time	明天我们几点见面？ What time shall we meet tomorrow?
半 bàn	n	half	现在十二点半了。 It is half past twelve now.
应该 yīnggāi	vt	should	你应该跟他道歉。 You should apologize to him.
个 gè	quant	classifier used before nouns that have no special quantifier	哪个人是一明？ Which person is Yi Ming?
哪个 nǎge	pron	which	哪个食堂？ Which canteen?

续表

生　词	词　性	解　释	举　例
楼 lóu	n	floor	我现在在三楼。 I am on the third floor.
几楼 jǐ lóu		which floor	餐厅在几楼? Which floor is the restaurant located?

汉字 Chinese Characters

独体字(dútǐzì) Single character

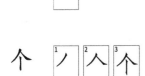

合体字(hétǐzì) Combined character

吃　左右结构 zuǒyòu jiégòu Left-right structure 口 乞

It is a signific-phonetic character. The left part 口 (mouth) is the signific element. It represents to eat. The right part 乞(qǐ) is the phonetic element. It represents the similar sound of the whole character. The primitive sense of 吃 means not speaking fluently. Its extended sense is to eat.

饭　左右结构 zuǒyòu jiégòu　Left-right structure　饣　反

It is a signific-phonetic character. The left part 饣（食，shí 食）is the signific element. It represents the food. The right part 反（fǎn）is the phonetic element. It represents the similar sound of the whole character. The primitive sense of 饭 means cooked rice. And its extended sense is food; meal.

现　左右结构 zuǒyòu jiégòu　Left-right structure　王　见

It is a signific-phonetic character. Also it is an ideographical structure. The left part 王 is 玉（yù）not Chinese family name 王（wáng）. 王（玉，yù）is the signific element. The right part 见（jiàn）is the phonetic element. It represents the similar sound of the whole character. The character describes polishing jade to show its brilliance. It means appear/show.

和　左右结构 zuǒyòu jiégòu　Left-right structure　禾　口

It is a signific-phonetic character. The left part 禾（hé）is the phonetic element. It represents the same sound of the whole character. The signific element is the right element 口（kǒu, speak）. It describes people speak harmoniously. The primitive sense is harmonious. The extended sense is and.

楼　左右结构 zuǒyòu jiégòu　Left-right structure　木　娄

It is a signific-phonetic character. The left part 木（mù, wood）is the signific element. The right part 娄（lóu）is the phonetic element. It represents the same sound of the whole character.

该 左右结构 zuǒyòu jiégòu Left-right structure 讠 亥

It is a signific-phonetic character. The left part is the signific element. The right part 亥 (hài) is the phonetic element. It represents the similar sound of the whole character.

食 上下结构 shàngxià jiégòu Upper-lower structure 人 良

The ancient writing is . It looks like some food in a container.

堂 上下结构 shàngxià jiégòu Upper-lower structure 𭥍 呈

It is a signific-phonetic character. The upper part 尚 (shàng) is the phonetic element. The lower part 土 (tǔ) is the signific element. Its primitive sense is tall house.

点 上下结构 shàngxià jiégòu Upper-lower structure 占 灬

Its signific element is 灬 which is the variant of the 火 (huǒ, fire). Some Chinese characters that contain this radical are all related to fire, for example 热 (rè, hot)、熟 (shú, cooked; done)、煎 (jiān, fry), etc. The original meaning of the word "点" means the black spot left by a fire. And now it means small blobs, for example 雨点 (raindrops), etc. Its phonetic element is 占 (zhàn).

应 左上包围结构 zuǒshàng bāowéi jiégòu Left-top surrounding structure 广 丷

📋 注释 Notes

时间　Time

时　间	拼　音	英　文	时　间	拼　音	英　文
0 点	língdiǎn	zero o'clock	1 分	yìfēn	one minute
1 点	yīdiǎn	one o'clock	2 分	èrfēn	two minutes
2 点	liǎngdiǎn	two o'clock	3 分	sānfēn	three minutes
3 点	sāndiǎn	three o'clock	4 分	sìfēn	four minutes
4 点	sìdiǎn	four o'clock	5 分	wǔfēn	five minutes
5 点	wǔdiǎn	five o'clock	6 分	liùfēn	six minutes
6 点	liùdiǎn	six o'clock	7 分	qīfēn	seven minutes
7 点	qīdiǎn	seven o'clock	8 分	bāfēn	eight minutes
8 点	bādiǎn	eight o'clock	9 分	jiǔfēn	nine minutes
9 点	jiǔdiǎn	nine o'clock	10 分	shífēn	ten minutes
10 点	shídiǎn	ten o'clock	11 分	shíyīfēn	eleven minutes
11 点	shíyīdiǎn	eleven o'clock	15 分	shíwǔfēn	fifteen minutes
12 点	shíèrdiǎn	twelve o'clock	30 分	sānshífēn	thirty minutes
几点	jǐdiǎn	what time	45 分	sìshíwǔfēn	forty five minutes
			几分	jǐfēn	what minute(s)

💬 语法 Grammar

语气助词"吧"　The modal particle "吧"

表示要求、商量的语气。例如：

Express the tone of request and discussion, e.g.

1. 我们一起吃饭吧。

2. 去公园踢球吧。

3. 星期六，我们一起去玩儿吧。

人称代词"咱们" The personal pronoun "咱们"

人称代词，指自己与别人，表示复数。例如：

Personal pronouns refer to oneself and others, e.g.

1. 咱们走吧。

2. 咱们一起去吧。

3. 咱们去哪个食堂吃饭？

练习 Exercises

一、听后选择正确的读音 Listen and choose the correct pronunciation

1. (　　) A. chīfàn　　　　 B. cīfàn　　　　 C. chǐfàn

2. (　　) A. xiànzài　　　　 B. xiànzhài　　　 C. xiānzài

3. (　　) A. jǐ diǎn　　　　 B. jí dián　　　　 C. jǐ diàn

4. (　　) A. tiānqì　　　　 B. tiānqí　　　　 C. tiànqì

5. (　　) A. shítáng　　　　 B. sítang　　　　 C. shítang

二、选择所给词语的正确读音 Choose the correct pronunciation of the words given

1. (　　) 食堂　 A. shítáng　　 B. sítang　　　 C. shítán

2. (　　) 吃饭　 A. cīfàn　　　 B. chīfàn　　　 C. chīfàn

3. (　　) 现在　 A. xiànzài　　 B. xiánzài　　　 C. xiànzāi

4. (　　) 应该　 A. yīngāi　　　 B. yīnggā　　　 C. yīnggāi

5. (　　) 几楼　 A. jǐ lóu　　　 B. jǐ ló　　　　 C. jí lóu

6. (　　) 几点　 A. jǐ diǎn　　 B. jí diǎn　　　 C. jǐ dǎn

三、请用下列词语填空 Please fill in the blanks with the following words

A. 几点　　 B. 食堂　　 C. 几楼　　 D. 太　　 E. 一会儿　　 F. 应该

例如：现在是(A)？

1. 我们去(　　　　)吃饭吧。

2. 食堂在(　　　　　)？

3. 我想等(　　　　　)再去吃饭，我还不饿。

4. 现在是 12 点半，食堂人(　　　　　)少了，咱们走吧。

5. 现在食堂里的人(　　　　　)多了，我们等一会儿再去吧。

四、汉字练习 Chinese character practice

1. 找出现代汉字对应的古代汉字 Match the ancient Chinese characters and the modern Chinese characters

多　　　　　　　　

饭　　　　　　　　

食

2. 分析下列汉字的结构 Analyze the structure of the following Chinese characters

该　楼　多　和　堂　现

左右结构 Left-right structure _____

上下结构 Upper-lower structure _____

3. 写出下列汉字的笔画 Write the strokes of the following Chinese characters

多_____

少_____

点_____

楼_____

和_____

食_____

五、书写练习 Writing exercises

1. 书写汉字 Writing Chinese characters

例如：我 jiào（叫）小米。

（1）我要去吃 fàn(　　　　　)。

（2）食堂里的人好 duō(　　　　　)。

（3）现在几 diǎn(　　　　　)了。

（4）现在食堂的人应 gāi(　　　　　)少了。

（5）等一 huìr(　　　　　)，我马上来。

2. 按正确的顺序组合句子并书写在横线上 Assemble the sentences in the correct order and write them on the line

例如：叫　我　大山

我叫大山。

(1)点　几　现在

_____

(2)食堂　去　吃饭　你　吗

_____

(3)人　食堂　多　太　现在　了

_____

(4)天气　今天　好　很

_____

(5)我　你　和　一起　食堂　去　吃饭

_____

六、课堂活动 Class activities

两人一组互相询问一天的时间安排。

Two people ask each other about the schedule of the day.

第八课　今天星期几?
Lesson 8　What day is it today?

📅 课文 Text

课文一　Text 1

在食堂，一明、大山、小米相约吃午饭，大江有事没来。

In the canteen, Yi Ming, Da Shan and Xiao Mi meet for lunch, but Da Jiang does not come.

（大山、小米先买好饭，找到位置坐下，边聊边等待一明。）

（Da Shan and Xiao Mi buy their meals first, find a seat and sit down, chatting and waiting for Yi Ming.）

大山：今天星期几?

小米：今天星期五，有什么事情吗?

大山：星期六，我们一起去玩儿吧。

小米：好的，去哪儿玩呢?

大山：去公园玩吧。

小米：好的。

课文二　Text 2

（一明走了过来。）

（Yi Ming comes over.）

小米：明天星期六，你有事情吗?

一明：没有。

小米：我们一起去公园玩儿吧。

一明：好的。

课文三 Text 3

今天是星期五，明天是星期六，大山、小米、一明明天去公园玩。

📝 生词 New Words

生　词	词　性	解　　释	举　例
今天 jīntiān	n	today	今天是星期日。 Today is Sunday.
明天 míngtiān	n	tomorrow	明天是我的生日。 Tomorrow is my birthday.
星期 xīngqī	n	week	这雪将会下一个星期。 The snow will last for a week.
星期几 Xīngqī jǐ		ask about the day	今天星期几? What day is it today?
星期五 Xīngqīwǔ	n	Friday	今天星期五。 It's Friday today.
星期六 Xīngqīliù	n	Saturday	今天是星期六。 Today is Saturday.
有 yǒu	vt	have	我有机会夺得冠军。 I have the chance to win the champion.
事情 shìqing	n	affair; matter work; job	明天我有点事情。 I have some job to do tomorrow.
一起 yìqǐ	adv	together; in company	我们要一起去远足。 We will go hiking together.
去 qù	vt	go to; leave for	我要去上海。 I will go to Shanghai.
哪儿 nǎr	pron	where	你要去哪儿? Where are you going?

续表

生　词	词　性	解　释	举　例
玩 wán	vt	play；have fun；amuse oneself	今天我去公园玩了。 I went to the park and play today.
玩儿 wánr	vt	play；have fun；amuse oneself. We usually add er after the vowel which is called Erhua. And it is a common phenomenon in Chinese. It doesn't change the meaning of the word. But it can convey a relaxed and lively tone not very formal.	你明天去哪儿玩儿？ Where are you going to play tomorrow？
吧 ba	modal particle	imperative mood	我们一块去吃晚饭吧！ Let's go for dinner！
公园 gōngyuán	n	park	在学校附近有一个公园。 There is a park near the school.

汉字 Chinese Characters

独体字(dútǐzì)　Single character

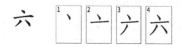

有　

公　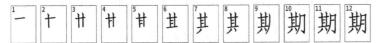

合体字(hétǐzì)　Combined character

期　左右结构 zuǒyòu jiégòu　Left-right structure　其　月

It is a signific-phonetic character. The left part 其(qí) is the phonetic element. The right part 月(moon) is the signific element which means month. 期 means the date.

情　左右结构 zuǒyòu jiégòu　Left-right structure　忄　青

It is a signific-phonetic character. The left part 忄 is a variant of 心 (xīn, heart), it is the signific element. The right part 青 (qīng) is the phonetic element and its pronunciation is similar to 情.

玩　左右结构 zuǒyòu jiégòu　Left-right structure　王　完

It is a signific-phonetic character. 王(玉, yù, jade) is the signific element, and 元 (yuán) is the phonetic element.

吧　左右结构 zuǒyòu jiégòu　Left-right structure　口　巴

It is a signific-phonetic character. 口 is the signific element, 巴 is the phonetic element.

It is a modal auxiliary.

星　上下结构 shàngxià jiégòu　Upper-lower structure　日　生

Its ancient writing is  just like the stars are rising. The upper part 日 is the star not the sun. The lower part 生（shēng）means appear or arise. It is an ideograph.

起　左下包围结构 zuǒxià bāowéi jiégòu　Lower-left Surrounding structure　走　己

It is a signific-phonetic character. 走（zǒu，go）is signific element，己（jǐ，oneself）is the phonetic element. Its primitive sense is to stand up.

园　全包围结构 quán bāowéi jiégòu　Complete Surrounding structure　囗　元

It is a signific-phonetic character. 囗 wéi means someplace. 元（yuan）represents the pronunciation of 园.

注释 Notes

星期　Week

星期一	星期二	星期三	星期四	星期五	星期六	星期日	星期几
Xīngqīyī	Xīngqīèr	Xīngqīsān	Xīngqīsì	Xīngqīwǔ	Xīngqīliù	Xīngqīrì	Xīngqī jǐ
Monday	Tuesday	Wednesday	Thursday	Friday	Saturday	Sunday	What day

其他表示时间的词语　Other words that mean time

前天	昨天	今天	明天	后天	每天
qiántiān	zuótiān	jīntiān	míngtiān	hòutiān	měitiān
the day before yesterday	yesterday	today	tomorrow	the day after tomorrow	every day
前天早晨	昨天早晨	今天早上	明天早晨	后天早晨	每天早上
qiántiān zǎochen	zuótiān zǎochen	jīntiān zǎoshang	míngtiān zǎochen	hòutiān zǎochen	měitiān zǎoshang
The morning before yesterday	yesterday morning	this morning	tomorrow morning	the morning after tomorrow	every morning
前天晚上	昨天晚上	今天晚上	明天晚上	后天晚上	每天晚上
qiántiān wǎnshang	zuótiān wǎnshang	jīntiān wǎnshang	míngtiān wǎnshang	hòutiān wǎnshang	měitiān wǎnshang
the evening before yesterday	yesterday evening	this evening	tomorrow evening	the evening after tomorrow	every evening
上上个星期	上个星期	这个星期	下个星期	下下个星期	每个星期
shàngshàng gèxīngqī	shànggè xīngqī	zhègè xīngqī	xiàgè xīngqī	xiàxiàgè xīngqī	měigè xīngqī
the week before last week	last week	this week	next week	the week after next week	every week
上上个月	上个月	这个月	下个月	下下个月	每个月
shàngshàng gèyuè	shànggèyuè	zhègèyuè	xiàgèyuè	xiàxiàgèyuè	měigèyuè
the month before last month	last month	this month	next month	the month after next month	every month

🗩 语法 Grammar

名词谓语句 The sentence with a nominal predicate

名词谓语句是名词性词语充当谓语的句子，一般用于表达年龄、时间、日期、天气等。例如：

Noun-predicate sentences are sentences in which nominal words serve as predicates, and are generally used to express age, time, date, e.g.

1. 王老师 30 岁。
2. 今天星期二。
3. 明天 22 号。
4. 明天晴天。

疑问词"哪儿" The question word "哪儿"

"哪儿"是疑问代词，用于疑问句中，询问人或事物的位置。例如：

"哪儿" is an interrogative pronoun, used in interrogative sentences to ask about the position of people or things, e.g.

1. 星期天，你去哪儿?
2. 汉语书在哪儿?
3. 你的汉语老师在哪儿?
4. 你的中国朋友在哪儿?

🗐 练习 Exercises

一、听后选择正确的读音 Listen and choose the correct pronunciation

1. (   ) A. jīntiān   B. jīngtiān   C. jìntiān

2. (   ) A. xīngqīn   B. xīnqīn   C. xīngqī

3. (   ) A. shìqing   B. sìqíng   C. sìqing

4. (   ) A. míntiān   B. míngtiān   C. míngtián

5. (   ) A. yìqǐ   B. yìqì   C. yíqǐ

二、选择所给词语的正确读音 Choose the correct pronunciation of the words given

1. (　　) 事情　A. shìqing　　B. sìqing　　　　C. sìqin

2. (　　) 公园　A. gōuyuán　　B. gōngyuán　　C. gòngyuán

3. (　　) 一起　A. yìqǐ　　　　B. yīqǐn　　　　C. yīnqǐ

4. (　　) 星期　A. xìngqī　　　B. xīngqīn　　　C. xīngqī

5. (　　) 今天　A. jīngtiān　　B. jīntiān　　　C. jīntián

三、请用下列词语填空 Please fill in the blanks with the following words

　　A. 星期六　　B. 一起　　C. 事情　　D. 公园　　E. 没有　　F. 几

例如：今天是(　A　)。

1. 明天星期(　　　)

2. A：你今天晚上有(　　　)吗？

　　B：(　　　)。

3. 我们(　　　)出去玩吧。

4. 我们去(　　　)走一走吧。

四、汉字练习 Chinese character practice

　　1. 找出现代汉字对应的古代汉字 Match the ancient Chinese characters and the modern Chinese characters

事

玩

星

2. 分析下列汉字的结构 Analyze the structure of the following Chinese characters

　　　　吧　　几　　星　　玩　　公　　情　　五　　园

左右结构 Left-right structure _____

上下结构 Upper-lower structure _____

包围结构 Three-sided surrounding structure _____

独体字 Single character _____

　　3. 写出下列汉字的笔画 Write the strokes of the following Chinese characters

好 _____

玩 _____

星 _____

期 _____

事 _____

五、书写练习 Writing exercises

1. 书写汉字 Writing Chinese characters

例如：今天 Xīng（星）期六

（1）我们去 wán（   ）吧。

（2）明天星期 jǐ（   ）？

（3）我们一 qǐ（   ）去吃饭吧。

（4）你今天晚上有 shì（   ）情吗？

（5）星期天天气好，我们一起去公 yuán（   ）吧。

2. 按正确的顺序组合句子并书写在横线上 Assemble the sentences in the correct order and write them on the line

例如：叫　我　大山

　　　我叫大山。

（1）星期　几　今天

_____

（2）去　我们　公园　玩　吧

_____

（3）有　事情　你　今天　吗

_____

（4）我们　食堂　一起　去　吧

_____

（5）星期三　我们　汉语　课　有

_____

六、课堂活动 Class activities

两人一组，邀请朋友星期天外出游玩。

As a group of two, invite friends to go out on Sunday.

第九课　你去哪儿?
Lesson 9　Where are you going?

📅 课文 Text

课文一　Text 1

在公寓，大山和小米晚饭后，在大厅遇到时的对话。

In the apartment, the conversation between Da Shan and Xiao Mi when they meet in the hall after dinner.

（大山背着书包正往外面走，小米刚从外面来到大厅。）

(Da Shan is walking outside with his school bag on his back, and Xiao Mi has just come to the hall from outside.)

小米：你去哪儿?

大山：我去图书馆，你去吗?

小米：是去借书吗?

大山：不是借书，是还书。

小米：哦，我不去。

课文二　Text 2

（大山从图书馆回来，正看到小米从楼梯上下来。）

(Da Shan is coming back from the library when he see Xiao Mi coming down the stairs.)

大山：你去哪儿?

小米：我去电影院看电影，你去吗?

大山：什么电影?

小米：《你好，李焕英》，据说，电影很好。

大山：几点开始？

小米：晚上8点半开始。还差半小时，快一点儿。

大山：好的，等我一下儿。

课文三　Text 3

晚饭后，大山去图书馆还书，回来后，我小米一起去电影院看电影。

☑ 生词 New Words

生　词	词　性	解　　释	举　　例
图书馆 túshūguǎn	n	library	我去图书馆。 I'm going to the library.
借书 jiè shū		to check out books	我去图书馆借书了。 I go to the library to check out books.
还书 huán shū		to return a book	我去图书馆还书。 I go to the library to return the books.
电影 diànyǐng	n	film; movie; motion picture	这部电影非常好看。 This movie is really great.
院 yuàn	n	courtyard; yard; compound	医院 hospital
电影院 diànyǐngyuàn	n	cinema; movie theatre; movie/picture house	公园旁边有一个电影院。 There is a cinema next to the park.
据说 jùshuō	v	it is said/alleged（that）; they say（that）; I hear	这家餐厅据说很好吃。 It is said that this restaurant is great.
很 hěn	adv	very; quite; awfully	这项任务完成得很好。 The task is finished very well.

生 词	词 性	解 释	举 例
很好 hěn hǎo		very good	他的英语水平很好。 His English skill is very good.
开始 kāishǐ	vt	begin；start；commence	电影九点开始。 The movie starts at 9 o'clock.
晚上 wǎnshang	n	evening；night	我们晚上要去玩游戏。 We will go to play games in the evening.
还 hái	adv	still；yet	我还没想好中午吃什么。 I haven't figured out what to eat for lunch yet.
差 chà	v	differ from；fall short of	他们的性格有差异。 Their characters differ from each other.
还差 hái chà		still differ from /fall short of	电影还差半小时开始。 The movie still needs half an hour to start.
快 kuài	adj	fast；quick	这辆车的速度非常快。 The car is really fast.
一点儿 yìdiǎnr	adj	a bit；a little	快一点儿。 Hurry up a bit.
等 děng	vt	wait for；await	请稍等我十分钟。 Please wait for me for 10 minutes.
一下儿 yíxiàr	adv	in a short while	等一下(儿) wait a minute
小时 xiǎoshí	n	hour	已经过去了一小时。 An hour has passed.
半小时 bànxiǎoshí	n	half an hour	这场球赛已经开始了半小时。 The game has started for half an hour.

 汉字 Chinese Characters

独体字 (dútǐzì) Single character

书　一　丂　书　书

电　丨　冂　冃　电　电

小　亅　小　小

Its ancient writing is 小 like three very small dots means small.

开　一　二　开　开

Its ancient writing is 闢. 門 means the door. ━ means the door latch. And 廾 like our two hands. The character looks like opening the latch with your hands means open.

半　丶　丷　丷　半　半

Its ancient writing is 半, 牛 means cow,)(means divide or separate.

The character looks like splitting a cow in half from the middle which means half.

合体字 (hétǐzì) Combined character

馆　左右结构 zuǒyòu jiégòu Left-right structure　饣 官

It is a signific-phonetic character. 饣 (食, shí) means to eat or food. It is the signific element. The Chinese characters that contain this radical are all related to eating, for example 饭（fàn, cooked rice; food, meal）、饮（yǐn, drink; swallow）、饥饿（jī'è, hunger; starvation）etc. 官（guān）is the phonetic element, the initial and final for both are the same, but the tone is different.

借　左右结构 zuǒyòu jiégòu　Left-right structure　亻　昔

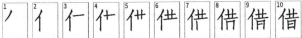

It is a signific-phonetic character. Signific element（left side）-亻（人, rén）, it represents human. Phonetic element（right side）-昔（xī）. it means formerly, in beginning. The initial, the final and the tones are all different. But in ancient Chinese the sound of 昔 is the same as 借.

影　左右结构 zuǒyòu jiégòu　Left-right structure　景　彡

It is a signific-phonetic character. Signific element（right side）彡（shān）means decorative pattern. Phonetic element（left side）景（jǐng）means scenery, view. The final and tone are the same, but their initials are different.

院　左右结构 zuǒyòu jiégòu　Left-right structure　阝　完

It is a signific-phonetic character. Its signific element（right side）is 阝（阜, fù, place）. Its phonetic element is 完（wán, complete, finish, settle; whole）The final is the same as /an/, but the initials and tones are different.

据　左右结构 zuǒyòu jiégòu　Left-right structure　扌　居

It is a signific-phonetic character. Its signific element（left side）is 手（shǒu, hand）. Its phonetic element is 居（jū, live, dwell, reside, sit）. The final and initial is the same, but the tones is different. The tone of 据 is falling, and the tone of 居 is high-level.

很 左右结构 zuǒyòu jiégòu Left-right structure 彳 艮

It is a signific-phonetic character. Its signific element (left side) is 彳 (chì, walk). Its phonetic element is 艮 (gèn). The final is /en/ for 艮 and 很, but the initial and the tone are different. The tone of 很 is falling-rising, and the tone of 艮 is falling.

始 左右结构 zuǒyòu jiégòu Left-right structure 女 台

It is a signific-phonetic character. Its signific element (left side) is 女 (nǔ, female). Its phonetic element is 台 (tái). The final, the initial and the tone are all different.

晚 左右结构 zuǒyòu jiégòu Left-right structure 日 免

It is a signific-phonetic character. Its signific element (left side) is 日 (rì, sun; day; daytime). Its phonetic element is 免 (miǎn, spare; evade;. avoid). The final, the initial and the tone are all different.

时 左右结构 zuǒyòu jiégòu Left-right structure 日 寸

It is a signific-phonetic character. Its signific element is 日 which means sun; day; daytime. The Chinese characters that contain this radical are all related to time, for example 晚、昨 (yesterday)、早 (morning), etc.

等 上下结构 shàngxià jiégòu Upper-lower structure 竹 寺

It is an ideograph. Its primitive sense is to put the books in order. Its extended sense are as follows：equal；etc；rank，etc.

还　左下包围结构 zuǒxià bāowéi jiégòu　Lower-left Surrounding structure　辶 不

¹ 一	² 丁	³ 不	⁴ 不	⁵ 环	⁶ 还	⁷ 还

It is a signific-phonetic character. The original meaning of the word 还 means go back to where you are. 还 is the simplified character of 還, 不（bù，not）is the simplified character of 瞏. 瞏（huán）is the phonetic element. 辶（chuò，walk）is the signific element.

注释 Notes

建筑设施　Building and facilities

中　文	英　文	拼　音
大楼	building	dà lóu
电影院	cinema	diànyǐngyuàn
美术馆	art gallery	měishùguǎn
体育馆	stadium	tǐyùguǎn
博物馆	museum	bówùguǎn
图书馆	library	túshūguǎn
公园	park	gōngyuán
动物园	zoo	dòngwùyuán
植物园	botanical garden	zhíwùyuán
游乐园	amusement park	yóulèyuán
车站	station	chēzhàn
机场	airport	jīchǎng
消防局	fire department	xiāofángjú
警察局	police office	jǐngchájú

续表

中 文	英 文	拼 音
派出所	police station	pàichūsuǒ
医院	hospital	yīyuàn
银行	bank	yínháng
邮局	post office	yóujú
工厂	factory	gōngchǎng
停车场	parking lot	tíngchēchǎng
学校	school	xuéxiào
商店	shop	shāngdiàn
书店	bookstore	shūdiàn
理发店	barber shop	lǐfàdiàn
药店	pharmacy	yàodiàn
咖啡馆	coffee shop	kāfēiguǎn
宾馆	hotel	bīnguǎn
超市	supermarket	chāoshì
饭店	restaurant	fàndiàn
水果店	fruit shop	shuǐguǒdiàn
洗衣店	laundry	xǐyīdiàn

语法 Grammar

形容词谓语句　Adjective predicates

形容词性词语充当谓语的句子叫形容词谓语句，一般用于表达年龄、时间、日期等。肯定形式中，形容词前常常用程度副词"很"，否定形式要在形容词前加上否定副词"不"。

Sentences in which adjective words serve as predicates are called adjective predicates, which are generally used to express age, time, and date. In the positive form, the degree adverb "very" is often used before the adjective, and the negative adverb "no" is added before the adjective in the negative form.

肯定形式的语序：主语+副词+形容词

Positive form of word order：Subject + Adverb + Adjective，e.g.

1. 天气很好。

2. 专业很好。

3. 他的汉语很好。

否定形式的语序：主语+不+形容词

Negative word order：Subject+不+ Adjective，e.g.

1. 天气不好。

2. 专业不好。

3. 他的汉语不好。

数量词"一点儿"　The quantifier "一点儿"

"一点儿"用在形容词后边，表示比较。例如：

When used after an adjective , it shows comparison，e.g.

1. 还差半小时，快一点儿。

2. 这件衣服，我要大一点儿的。

3. 这件衣服短了一点儿，有长一点儿的吗?

数量词"一下(儿)"　The quantifier "一下(儿)"

"一下(儿)"用于短时间的行为后，有缓和语气的作用。例如：

"一下(儿)"means a bit. "Verb +一下(儿)" implies a short and quick action. It is often used to soften the tone，e.g.

1. 等我一下儿。

2. 借一下你的书。

3. 我看一下几点了。

🔖 练习 Exercises

一、听后选择正确的读音 Listen and choose the correct pronunciation

1. (　　) A. nǎli　　　　　B. nàlì　　　　　C. lā lì

2. (　　) A. shōují　　　　B. shújì　　　　　C. shǒujī

3. (　　) A. huán shū　　　B. diànyǐng　　　C. jùshuō

4. (　　) A. hěn hǎo　　　B. kāishǐ　　　　C. wǎnshang

5. (　　) A. xiǎoshí　　　　　B. hái chà　　　　C. jiè shū

二、选择所给词语的正确读音 Choose the correct pronunciation of the words given

1. (　　)电影　A. diànyǐng　　　B. diànyǐn　　　C. dànyǐng
2. (　　)很好　A. hènhǎo　　　　B. hěnhào　　　C. hěnhǎo
3. (　　)晚上　A. wǎnshang　　　B. wǎshang　　　C. wǎnshan
4. (　　)还差　A. háicà　　　　　B. háichà　　　C. háchà
5. (　　)小时　A. xiǎoshí　　　　B. xiǎosí　　　C. xiàoshí
6. (　　)据说　A. jùshuō　　　　B. jùsuō　　　C. jùshuò

三、请用下列词语填空 Please fill in the blanks with the following words

A. 图书馆　　　B. 电影院　　　C. 很好　　　D. 据说　　　E. 还书　　　F. 一点儿
例如：我今天要去(E)

1. 我要去(　　　　　)借书。
2. 这本书(　　　　　)看。
3. 这部电影很好看，我们一起去(　　　　　)看吧。
4. 这件衣服长了(　　　　　)，不太合适。
5. (　　　　　)明天天气很好，我们一起去公园玩儿吧。

四、汉字练习 Chinese character practice

1. 找出现代汉字对应的古代汉字 Match the ancient Chinese characters and the modern Chinese characters

开　　　　　　伞

半　　　　　　八

门　　　　　　門

小　　　　　　闢

2. 分析下列汉字的结构 Analyze the structure of the following Chinese characters

点　　还　　等　　晚　　院

左右结构 Left-right structure _____

上下结构 Upper-lower structure _____

左下包围结构 Lower-left surrounding structure _____

3. 写出下列汉字的笔画 Write the strokes of the following Chinese characters

院 _____

很 _____

电 _____

差 _____

还 _____

五、书写练习 Writing exercises

1. 书写汉字 Writing Chinese characters

例如：我 jiào（叫）小米。

（1）我要去 jiè（   ）书。

（2）jù（   ）说这部电影很好看。

（3）电影三点钟 kāi（   ）始。

（4）我去图书馆 huán（   ）书，你去吗？

（5）děng（   ）一下儿，我先去上课，回来和你联系。

2. 按正确的顺序组合句子并书写在横线上 Assemble the sentences in the correct order and write them on the line

例如：叫   我   大山

      我叫大山。

（1）半小时   差   还   上课

_____

（2）电影   看   一起   去   吗

_____

（3）图书馆   我   借书   去

_____

（4）一下儿   等   电影院   去

_____

（5）一起   晚上   朋友   和   食堂   去   吃饭

_____

六、课堂活动 Class activities

两人一组，互相询问周日去哪儿玩儿。

Make a group of two and ask each other where to go on Sunday.

第十课 你在干什么?

Lesson 10   What are you doing?

📅 课文 Text

课文一   Text 1

在公寓,大山给小米打电话,想邀请小米一起去商场购物。

In the apartment, Da Shan calls Xiao Mi and wants to invite Xiao Mi to go shopping at the mall together.

(大山给小米打电话,始终占线。大山于是去敲小米的门,小米来开门。)

(Da Shan called Xiao Mi, but the line was always busy. Da Shan then go to knock on Xiao Mi's door and Xiao Mi comes to open it.)

大山:小米,你在干什么呢? 为什么不接电话?

小米:对不起,我手机静音了,没听见。

大山:哦,没关系。

小米:你有什么事吗?

大山:我去沃尔玛买东西,你去吗?

小米:去,我也想去买点儿东西。

大山:我在楼下等你。

小米:好的。

课文二   Text 2

(大山在公寓楼下等小米,一刻钟过去了,小米还没来,大山又给小米打电话。)

(Da Shan waits for Xiao Mi downstairs, a quarter of an hour has passed and Xiao Mi hasn't come, so Da Shan calls Xiao Mi again.)

大山：你在干什么呢？为什么还没下楼？

小米：我在找钥匙，我的钥匙不知道放哪里了？

大山：哦，不急，慢慢儿找吧，我等你。

小米：啊！找到了。

课文三　Text 3

大山给小米打电话，小米的手机因为静音，没有听见。

大山去找小米，想和她一起去沃尔玛买东西。

生词 New Words

生　词	词　性	解　释	举　例
在 zài	prep	in；be；at	你在哪儿？ Where are you?
公寓 gōngyù	n	apartment	他在公寓。 He's in the apartment.
干什么 gàn shénme		do what?	你在干什么？ What are you doing?
电话 diànhuà	n	telephone；phone	我们电话联系。 Let's contact by phone.
接 jiē	vt	to get；to receive	我接了一个任务。 I receive a task.
接电话 jiē diànhuà		answer the phone	他在接电话。 He's on the phone.
妈妈 māma	n	mom；mama	这是我妈妈。 This is my mom.
对不起 duì bu qǐ	adj	sorry	对不起，我来晚了。 Sorry, I'm late.

续表

生　词	词　性	解　释	举　例
手机 shǒujī	n	cellphone	每个人都有手机。 Everyone has a cellphone.
静音 jìngyīn	adj	mute	我把手机静音了。 I muted my phone.
听见 tīngjiàn	v	hear	你能听见我说话吗？ Can you hear me?
想 xiǎng	vt	want to; would like to	我想回家。 I want to go home.
买 mǎi	vt	buy	我们去买书吧！ Let's buy some books!
东西 dōngxi	n	thing	商场里有很多东西。 There are many things in the market.
楼下 lóu xià	n	downstairs	我在楼下等你。 I'm waiting for you downstairs.
下来 xiàlái	vi	come down; come from a higher place	我才从楼上下来。 I just came down from upstairs.
找 zhǎo	vt	discover; seek; look for	我在找一个人。 I'm looking for someone.
找到 zhǎo dào	vt	find; seek out	我找到了丢失的钱包。 I found the lost wallet.
钥匙 yàoshi	n	key	用钥匙开门。 Open the door with the key.
知道 zhīdào	vt	know	你知道孔子吗？ Do you know Confucius?

续表

生　词	词　性	解　释	举　例
放 fàng	vt	put；place	把书放桌上。 Put the book on the table.
哪里 nǎlǐ	adv	where	你来自哪里？ Where are you from?
急 jí	adj	worried	要迟到了我很急。 I'm worried that I'm going to be late.
不急 bù jí		take your time, no hurry	不急，现在还早。 No hurry, it's still early.
慢慢儿 mànmānr	adv	slowly；gradually	慢慢儿找，不着急。 Take your time searching, don't worry.
啊 à	int	ah；oh	啊！我中奖了！ Ah! I won the prize!
给 gěi	prep	for；to	给你钥匙。 Here's the key for you.

汉字 Chinese Characters

独体字(dútǐzì)　Single character

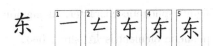

西

合体字(hétǐzì)　Combined character

静　左右结构 zuǒyòu jiégòu　Left-right structure　青　争

It is a significic-phonetic character. Its significic element is 争(zhēng, contend; dispute). Its phonetic element is 青(qīng, green; blue). The final for 青 and 静 is the same, but the initial and tone are different.

慢　左右结构 zuǒyòu jiégòu　Left-right structure　忄　曼

It is a significic-phonetic character. Its significic element(left side) is 忄(心, xīn, heart; intention). Its phonetic element is 曼(màn, graceful; prolonged).

钥　左右结构 zuǒyòu jiégòu　Left-right structure　钅　月

It is a significic-phonetic character. Its significic element(left side) is 钅(jīn, metals). Its phonetic element is 月(yuè, moon). 钥 can be read as /yuè/ and /yào/. In modern Chinese, it is often read as /yào/.

匙　左下包围结构 zuǒxià bāowéi jiégòu　Lower-left Surrounding structure　是　匕

匙 has two pronunciations. It can be read as /chí/, which means spoon. It also can be read as /shi/ in 钥匙, which means key. It is a significic-phonetic character. Its significic element is 匕(bǐ, an ancient type of spoon). Its phonetic element is 是(shì, be).

道 左下包围结构 zuǒxià bāowéi jiégòu Lower-left Surrounding structure 辶 首

It is an ideograph. It is composed of two pictographs, i. e. 辶 (chuò, walk) and 首 (shǒu, head), expressing person walks on the road. Its primitive sense is road.

📋 注释 Notes

一天的生活 Dailylife

中 文	拼 音	英 文
起床	qǐchuáng	get up
开窗	kāi chuāng	open window
洗脸	xǐ liǎn	wash face
刷牙	shuā yá	brush teeth
梳头	shū tóu	comb hair
穿衣服	chuān yīfu	wear clothes
沏茶，泡茶	qī chá, pào chá	make tea
喝茶	hē chá	drink tea
吃饭	chī fàn	eat
抽烟	chōu yān	smokes
看报纸	kàn bàozhǐ	read newspaper
穿鞋	chuān xié	wear shoes
关门	guānmén	close the door
锁门	suǒ mén	lock the door
扔垃圾	rēng lājī	throw rubbish

续表

中　文	拼　音	英　文
去教室	qù jiàoshì	go to the classroom
买车票	mǎi chēpiào	buy a ticket
看杂志	kàn zázhì	read magazine
听音乐	tīng yīnyuè	listen to music
发邮件	fā yóujiàn	send email
打电话	dǎ diànhuà	make a call
去银行	qù yínháng	go to bank
付款	fùkuǎn	payment
回家	huíjiā	come back home
开锁	kāi suǒ	unlock
开门	kāimén	open the door
脱鞋	tuō xié	take off shoes
脱衣服	tuō yīfu	undress
开灯	kāi dēng	turn on the lights
开电视	kāi diànshì	turn on the TV
做饭	zuò fàn	cook
洗澡	xǐzǎo	take a bath
淋浴	línyù	take a shower
洗头发	xǐ tóufà	wash hair
关窗	guān chuāng	close the window
关灯	guān dēng	turn off the lights
睡觉	shuìjiào	sleep

🗨 语法 Grammar

连谓句 Link-predicate sentences

连谓短语充当谓语或独立成句的句子叫连谓句。连谓句内部的几个谓词不管语义关系如何，大多是遵循时间先后顺序排列，即先出现的动作在前。这些谓词都可以分别跟同一个施事发生语义关系，即都是同一施事的几个动作。

Sentences in which conjoined predicates act as predicates or stand-alone sentences are called conjoined predicates. Regardless of the semantic relationship of the several predicates in the even-predicate sentence, the order of arrangement mostly follows chronological order, that is, the action that appears first is first. These predicates can all have a semantic relationship with the same agent, that is, they are all actions of the same agent.

表示目的 Purpose

主语 + 来/去 + 处所 + 动词短语

Subject + 来/去 + Place + Verbal phrase

妈妈　来　上海　看我。

我　　去　图书馆　借书。

他　　去　沃尔玛　买东西。

第一个动词后表示地点的宾语有时可以省略。

The object of the place after the first verb can sometimes be omitted.

语序：主语 + 来/去 + 动词短语

　　　Subject + 来/去 + Verbal phrase

例：妈妈　来　看我。

　　我　　去　借书。

　　他　　去　买东西。

表示方式 Representation

主语 + 动词短语1 + 动词短语2

Subject + Verbal phrase 1 + Verbal phrase 2

他　乘地铁　上学。

注意事项 Matters needing attention：

注意动词短语的顺序，表目的时，表目的的短语在后；表方式时，表方式时，表方式的短语在前。

Pay attention to the order of verb phrases. When expressing the purpose, the phrase expressing the purpose comes after; In table mode, the phrase of table mode comes first.

副词"在"　The adverb "在"

副词"在"用在动词前表示动作正在进行，句尾加语气词"呢"也可表示动作进行，"在"和"呢"可以同时使用。

The adverb "在" is used in front of a verb to indicate that an action is in progress. The addition of the modal particle "ni" at the end of a sentence can also indicate that an action is in progress.

A：你在干什么呢？

B：我在找护照(呢)。

练习 Exercises

一、听后选择正确的读音 Listen and choose the correct pronunciation

1. (　　) A. dòngshǒu　　　B. dǒngshì　　　C. dōngxi

2. (　　) A. yǎsī　　　　　B. yàoshì　　　　C. yàoshi

3. (　　) A. duì bù duì　　B. duìbuqǐ　　　C. duìbúzhù

4. (　　) A. a　　　　　　B. á　　　　　　C. ǎ

5. (　　) A. diànyǐng　　　B. diànhuà　　　C. dànshì

二、给词语选择正确图片 Listen and choose the right picture

A. 　　　　　B.

C. 　　　　　D.

1. 电话(　　)　　2. 手机(　　)　　3. 钥匙(　　)　　4. 妈妈(　　)

三、选择所给词语的正确读音 Choose the correct pronunciation of the words given

1. (　　)下来　A. xiālái　　　　B. xiàlái　　　　C. xiàolái

2. (　　)知道　A. zhīdào　　　　B. zhǐdǎo　　　　C. zìdǎo

3. (　　)听见　A. tǐjiǎn　　　　B. tīngjiàn　　　　C. tíngjiàn

4. (　　)买　　A. mǎi　　　　　B. mài　　　　　C. mái

5. (　　)静音　A. jīyīn　　　　B. jīnyín　　　　C. jìngyīn

四、请用下列词语填空 Please fill in the blanks with the following words

A. 手机　　B. 干什么　　C. 楼下　　D. 东西　　E. 对不起　　F. 今天　　G. 太

例如：我在(C)等你。

1. (　　　　　)是晴天。

2. 我想去沃尔玛买(　　　　　)。

3. A：你在(　　　　　)？为什么不接电话？

　　B：(　　　　　)，我手机静音了，没听见。

4. 你真是(　　　　　)慢了，我等你好久了。

5. 小米的(　　　　　)因为静音，没有听见。

五、汉字练习 Chinese character practice

1. 找出现代汉字对应的古代汉字 Match the ancient Chinese characters and the modern Chinese characters

上

买

手

下

2. 分析下列汉字的结构 Analyze the structure of the following Chinese characters

钥　　匙　　吃　　道　　起

左下包围结构 Lower-left Surrounding structure _____

左右结构 Left-right structure _____

3. 写出下列汉字的笔画 Write the strokes of the following Chinese characters

卖 _____

送 _____

付_____

给_____

六、书写练习 Writing exercises

1. 书写汉字 Writing Chinese characters

例如：我 jiào（叫）小米。

（1）à（　　　　）！找到了。

（2）大山给小米打（　　　　）diànhuà。

（3）我在 zhǎo（　　　　）钥匙，我的钥匙不知道放哪了？

（4）我不知道要买什么 dōngxi（　　　　）。

（5）duìbuqǐ（　　　　），我迟到了。

（6）在上课的时候，大家要把手机调 jìngyīn（　　　　）。

2. 按正确的顺序组合句子并书写在横线上 Assemble the sentences in the correct order and write them on the line

例如：叫 我 大山

　　　我叫大山。

（1）去过　你　中国　吗

_____

（2）在　你　等　楼下

_____

（3）有　什么　事　你　吗

_____

（4）终于　我　找到　书　我的　了

_____

（5）知道　你的　我　哪里　书包　放在　了

_____

（6）我　不知道　钥匙　我的　哪里了　放

_____

七、课堂活动 Class activities

两人一组互相询问去沃尔玛购物的经历。

The pair asked each other about the experience of shopping at Wal-Mart.

第十一课　这件衣服怎么样?
Lesson 11　How about this dress?

📅 课文 Text

课文一　Text 1

在服装店，留学生大山和小米一起逛服装店。

In the clothing store, international students Da Shan and Xiao Mi are shopping together.

（大山在旁边等待，小米挑选衣服，店员在旁边介绍。）

（Da Shan is waiting by the side, Xiao Mi selects clothes, and the shop assistant introduces to them.）

小米：请问，这件衣服我可以试试吗?

店员：可以，你穿多大尺寸?

小米：我穿 M 号。

店员：好的，请稍等。

课文二　Text 2

（小米去试衣服，大山在旁边等待。）

（Xiao Mi goes to try on clothes while Da Shan waits nearby.）

小米：大山，你看这件衣服怎么样?

大山：有一点儿小，不适合你。你试试这件粉色的吧。

小米：哦，这件漂亮。我试试这件吧。

店员：好的。

（小米再次去试衣间，试大山推荐的粉色裙子。）

（Xiaomi goes to the fitting room again to try on the pink skirt recommended by Da Shan.）

小米：大山，你看这件衣服怎么样？

大山：很漂亮！大小正好。

小米：谢谢！那么，我就买这一件了。

课文三　Text 3

大山和小米一起去买衣服。第一件衣服有点儿小，大山给她拿了一件粉色连衣裙，很漂亮，小米非常喜欢。

📝 生词 New Words

生　词	词　性	解　释	举　例
这 zhè	pron	this；it；these	这是我的鼻子。 This is my nose.
那 nà	pron	that；it；which	那是飞机。 That is a plane.
件 jiàn	quant	used to describe clothing, etc	我买了一件外套。 I bought a coat.
衣服 yīfu	n	clothes；dress	这件衣服。 This dress.
挑选 tiāoxuǎn	vt	select；pick；choose	挑选衣服 Choosing clothes
试试 shìshi	vt	have a try	试试这件衣服？ Try this dress on.
穿 chuān	vt	put on；wear；pierce through	今天穿什么衣服呢？ What should I wear today?
多大 duō dà	pron	how； what（ask for years/size, etc）	这个苹果有多大？ How big is this apple?

生 词	词 性	解 释	举 例
尺寸 chǐcùn	n	size	这条裙子什么尺寸? What is the size of this dress?
号 hào	n	size	我穿 M 号。 I wear size M.
稍等 shāoděng	vt	wait a moment; just a moment; hold on	稍等,我去查一下。 Wait a minute, I will check it out.
怎么样 zěnmeyàng	adv	how	这个地方怎么样? How about this place?
有点儿 yǒudiǎnr	adj	a little; a bit	我有点儿饿了。 I'm a little hungry.
小 xiǎo	adj	little; small	这件衣服有点儿小。 This dress is a bit small.
适合 shìhé	vt	suit	这件衣服适合你。 This dress is suitable for you.
粉色 fěnsè	n	pink	我喜欢粉色。 I like pink.
裙子 qúnzi	n	skirt	女孩们爱穿裙子。 Girls like to waer skirts.
漂亮 piàoliang	adj	pretty; beautiful	你真漂亮! You are so beautiful!
大小 dàxiǎo	n	size	衣服的大小合适吗? Is the size of the clothes suitable?
正 zhèng	adv	just	我正准备出门。 I'm about to go out.

续表

生　词	词　性	解　释	举　例
正好 zhènghǎo	adv	just right	粉色裙子大小正好。 The pink skirt is just the right size.
就 jiù	adv	just	这件衣服很漂亮，我就想买这件。 This dress is very beauti- ful, I just want to buy this one.
非常 fēicháng	adv	very	尺寸非常合适。 The size is very suitable.

汉字 Chinese Characters

独体字(dútǐzì)　Single character

衣

Its oracle script is 衤. The pictograph describes the shape of an ancient dress.

色

寸

合体字(hétǐzì)　Combined character

服　左右结构 zuǒyòu jiégòu　Left-right structure　月　殳

Its oracle script is 𝄞(殳). It is an ideograph composed of 𝄞(a person), and 𝄞(a hand). Its primitive meaning is to grasp a person with one hand and make him give in. Its bronze script is 𝄞, people add a radical 月(月, a boat). Modern Chinese character is written as 服.

裙　左右结构 zuǒyòu jiégòu　Left-right structure　衤　君

It is a signific-phonetic character. Its signific element(right side) is 衤(yī, clothing), its phonetic element is 君(jūn, ruler; governor). The final is the same as /un/, but the initials and tones are different. Its basic meaning is group or crowd.

漂　左右结构 zuǒyòu jiégòu　Left-right structure　氵　票

It is a signific-phonetic character. Its signific element is 氵(shuǐ, water), its phonetic element is 票(piào). Its primitive sense is to float. Its extended sense is high and faraway.

亮　上下结构 shàngxià jiégòu　Upper-lower structure　亠　几

It is an ideograph composed of 亠(高 gāo, tall; high) and 几(jī, table). It means high and bright.

常　上下结构 shàngxià jiégòu　Upper-lower structure　　尚　巾

It is a signific-phonetic character. Its signific element is 巾 (jīn, scarf ; kerchief), its phonetic element is 尚 (尚 shàng, revere ; venerate). The original meaning is skirt or clothes. Its extended sense is often.

穿　上下结构 shàngxià jiégòu　Upper-lower structure　　穴　牙

It is an ideograph composed of 穴(xué, hole ; cavity)and 牙(yá, tooth). It may mean that the mouse made a hole with its fangs. Its primitive sense is to pierce through or penetrate. Its extended sense is to dress.

💬 语法 Grammar

动词重叠"试试"　The verb reduplication "试试"

"试试"是单音节动词的重叠形式：动词+动词，表达动作时间短、尝试、轻微等意义，重叠的动词一般要读轻声，使用这一格式时，说话的语气显得轻松、客气、随便，一般用于口语。例如：

"试试" is the overlapping form of single-syllable verbs：Verb + Verb, which expresses the meaning of short action time, trial, and lightness. Overlapping verbs should generally be read softly. When this format is used, the tone of speech appears Relaxed, polite, and casual, generally used in spoken English, e.g.

1. 我想试试这件衣服。
2. 小米：请问，这件衣服我可以试试吗？
   店员：当然可以。

结构助词"的"　The structural particle "的"

"的"附在名词、代词、形容词、动词或词组后面构成"的"字短语，相当于一个名词。例如：

"的" is attached to a noun, pronoun, adjective, verb or phrase to form a "的" phrase, which is equivalent to a noune.g.

试试这件粉色的吧！ = 试试这件粉色的(裙子)吧！

红色的和粉色的都有。 = 红色的和粉色的(裙子)都有。

副词"有(一)点儿" The adverb "有(一)点儿"

"有一点儿"作状语，用在形容词前，多用于表达不如意的事情。例如：

"有一点儿" is used as an adverbial before an adjective; expressing that something is undesirable or dissatisfying, e.g.

有一点儿小   有一点儿大

有一点儿长   有一点儿短

有一点儿贵   有一点儿便宜

练习 Exercises

一、听后选择正确的读音 Listen and choose the correct pronunciation

1. (   ) A. yīfu   B. yìwù   C. yīfù

2. (   ) A. qūzhú   B. qúnzǔ   C. qúnzi

4. (   ) A. chǐcùn   B. cǐcì   C. cǐchù

3. (   ) A. zhènghào   B. zhènghǎo   C. zhēnhǎo

5. (   ) A. biǎolù   B. piàoliang   C. piāorán

二、选择所给词语的正确读音 Choose the correct pronunciation of the words given

1. (   ) 衣服   A. yìfù   B. yīfu   C. yífu

2. (   ) 粉色   A. fěnsè   B. fēnshè   C. fēishè

3. (   ) 试试   A. shìshi   B. shìshí   C. shísì

4. (   ) 尺寸   A. chǐcùn   B. cǐcūn   C. chīcù

5. (   ) 稍等   A. shādēng   B. sàdé   C. shāoděng

三、请用下列词语填空 Please fill in the blanks with the following words

A. 大小   B. 叫   C. 试试   D. 衣服   E. 粉色   F. 适合

例如：我（ B ）大山。

1. 这件衣服很（　　　　　）你。

2. 请问，这件衣服我可以（　　　　　）吗？

3. 你试试这件（　　　　　）的裙子吧。

4. A：你看这件（　　　　　）怎么样？

　　B：很漂亮！（　　　　　）正好。

四、汉字练习 Chinese character practice

1. 找出现代汉字对应的古代汉字 Match the ancient Chinese characters and the modern Chinese characters

衣

服

手

2. 分析下列汉字的结构 Analyze the structure of the following Chinese characters

亮　　试　　常　　就　　穿

左右结构 Left-right structure _____

上下结构 Upper-lower structure _____

3. 写出下列汉字的笔画 Write the strokes of the following Chinese characters

正 _____

漂 _____

亮 _____

粉 _____

衣 _____

服 _____

五、书写练习 Writing exercises

1. 书写汉字 Writing Chinese characters

例如：我 jiào（叫）小米。

（1）这件衣服很 piàoliang（　　　　　）

（2）这件衣服很 shìhé（　　　　　）你。

（3）你喜欢 nǎ（　　　　　）件衣服？

(4) 你 shìshi(   )这件衣服?

(5) 你穿多大 chǐcùn(   )的衣服?

2. 按正确的顺序组合句子并书写在横线上 Assemble the sentences in the correct order and write them on the line

例如: 叫　我　大山

　　　我叫大山。

(1) 穿　你　尺寸　的　多大　衣服

_____

(2) 怎么样　看　这件　你　衣服

_____

(3) 别的　这件　尺寸　还有　衣服　吗

_____

(4) 我　一条　裙子　粉色的　想要

_____

(5) 买的　这件　衣服　我　合适　很

_____

(6) 衣服　的　那件　有　贵　一点儿　价格

_____

六、课堂活动 Class activities

两人一组,分别扮演顾客和店员进行购物训练。

In pairs, play customers and shop assistants for shopping training.

第十二课 这件衣服多少钱?
Lesson 12 How much is this dress?

📅 课文 Text

课文一 Text 1

在服装店,小米想买一件粉色连衣裙,和大山一起与店员砍价。

At the clothing store, Xiao Mi wants to buy a pink dress, she and Da Shan bargain with the shop assistant together.

(小米拿着粉色连衣裙向店员走去。)

(Xiao Mi walks towards the shop assistant with the pink dress.)

小米:你好,请问这件衣服怎么卖?

店员:一件 500 元。

小米:太贵了。便宜一点儿吧,300 元怎么样?

店员:300 元太少了,不卖。可以打九折,你给 450 元吧。

小米:再便宜一点儿吧。

店员:对不起,不能再便宜了。

课文二 Text 2

(大山拿着小米的衣服和包走了过来。)

(Da Shan comes over with Xiao Mi's clothes and bag.)

大山:430 元吧,这个价格我们就买了。

店员:好吧,那么就 430 元吧。

大山:小米,怎么样?

小米:好的。

课文三 Text 3

小米和大山一起去买衣服，小米刚开始试的一件衣服有点儿小，不合适。后来看中了一件粉色裙子，大小正合适，很漂亮。但是价格太贵了，一件500元。和店员砍价后，花了430元。

✍ 生词 New Words

生　词	词　性	解　释	举　例
砍价 kǎn jià		bargain	砍价能让价格变低。 Bargaining can lower the price.
卖 mài	vt	sell	他在卖水果。 He is selling fruits.
元 yuán	quant	the monetary unit of China	这件衣服卖100元。 This dress sells for 100 yuan.
贵 guì	adj	expensive	钻石太贵了！ Diamonds are too expensive!
便宜 piányi	adj	inexpensive；cheap	旧书很便宜。 Old books are very cheap.
能 néng	vt	can；be able to；be capable of	我能游泳。 I can swim.
再 zài	adv	more	我能再喝一杯吗？ Can I have another drink？
打折 dǎ zhé		to give a discount	年底店铺都在打折。 The stores are on sale at the end of the year.
价格 jiàgé	n	price	价格能再便宜吗？ Can the price be any cheaper？

续表

生 词	词 性	解 释	举 例
服装店 fú zhuāng diàn	n	clothing shop	我们去逛服装店吧！ Let's go to the clothing store!
刚 gāng	adv	just	现在刚好吃中饭。 It's just lunch now.
合适 héshì	adj	suitable; appropriate; becoming fit	这条裙子合适吗？ Is this dress suitable?
后来 hòulái	adv	later; afterwards; then	后来我出国了。 Later, I went abroad.
看中 kànzhòng	vt	prefer; take a fancy to; feel satisfied	我看中这个戒指了。 I prefer this ring.
店员 diànyuán	n	salesclerk; clerk	店员很热情。 The clerk is very enthusiastic.
后 hòu	prep	after	打折后 after discount
花 huā	vt	spend; expend	花 400 元 spend 400 yuan

汉 汉字 Chinese Characters

独体字(dútǐzì) Single character

元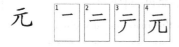

合体字(hétǐzì)　　Combined character

件　左右结构 zuǒyòu jiégòu　Left-right structure　亻　牛

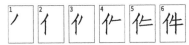

It is an ideograph. It is composed of two pictographs, i. e. 亻(人 rén, people)and 牛 (niú, cow), expressing person decomposes cattle. Its primitive sense is to decompose. Its extended senses are as follows: part; element; piece; article; item.

便　左右结构 zuǒyòu jiégòu　Left-right structure　亻　更

It is an ideograph. It is composed of two pictographs, i. e. 亻(人, rén, people)and 更 (gēng, change ; transform), expressing people are constantly changing to adapt to change. It can be read as /biàn/ and its primitive sense is convenient; easy, e.g. 方便. It can also be read as /pián/ which means inexpensive, e.g. 便宜.

刚　左右结构 zuǒyòu jiégòu　Left-right structure　冈　刂

It is a signific-phonetic character. Its signific element is 冈(gāng, ridge). Its phonetic element is 刂(刀, dāo, knife).

卖　上下结构 shàngxià jiégòu　Upper-lower structure　十　买

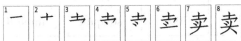

Its small seal script is 䙜. It is a signific-phonetic composed of signific element 屮 (出, chū, go out) and phonetic element 𧵅 (买, mǎi, buy). It means to sell. The final, the initial for 买 and 卖 are the same, but the tone is different.

装　上下结构 shàngxià jiégòu　Upper-lower structure　壮　衣

It is a signific-phonetic character. Its signific element is 衣(yī, clothes). Its phonetic element is 壮(zhuàng, spare; big, large). The final, the initial are the same, but the tone is different. Its primitive sense is outfit for a journey or luggage. Its extended senses are as follows: to pack things; clothes, etc.

花   上下结构 shàngxià jiégòu   Upper-lower structure   艹   化

It is a signific-phonetic character. Its signific element is 艹(cǎo, grass; plant). Its phonetic element is 化(huà, change). The final and the initial for 花 and 化 are the same, but the tone is different.

店   左上包围结构 zuǒshàng bāowéi jiégòu   Left-top Surrounding structure   广   占

It is a signific-phonetic character. Its signific element is 广(yǎn, a house built against a cliff). Its phonetic element is 占(zhàn, occupy). Its primitive sense is warehouse.

📋 注释 Notes

100 以上的数字   Numbers above 100

数　字	拼音	英　文	数　字	拼音	英　文
100	yībǎi	one hundred	2000	èrqiān	two thousand
200	èrbǎi	two hundred	3000	sānqiān	three thousand
300	sānbǎi	three hundred	4000	sìqiān	four thousand
400	sìbǎi	four hundred	5000	wǔqiān	five thousand
500	wǔbǎi	five hundred	6000	liùqiān	six thousand
600	liùbǎi	six hundred	7000	qīqiān	seven thousand
700	qībǎi	seven hundred	8000	bāqiān	eight thousand
800	bābǎi	eight hundred	9000	jiǔqiān	nine thousand

续表

数　字	拼　音	英　文	数　字	拼　音	英　文
900	jiǔbǎi	nine hundred	10000	yīwàn	ten thousand
1000	yīqiān	one thousand			

中国的钱　Chinese money

一元（yī yuán，one yuan）

五元（wǔ yuán，five yuan）

十元（shí yuán，ten yuan）

二十元（èrshí yuán，twenty yuan）

五十元（wǔshí yuán，fifty yuan）

一百元（yībǎi yuán，one hundred yuan）

🗨 语法 Grammar

副词"再" The adverb "再"

副词"再"放在动词前边作状语，表示尚未重复的动作或情况，例如：

The adverb "再" is placed before the verb as an adverbial, indicating an action or situation that has not been repeated, e.g.

店员：300元太少了，不卖。可以打九折，你给450元吧。

小米：再便宜一点儿吧。

店员：对不起，不能再便宜了。

能愿动词"能" The optative verb "能"

能愿动词"能"一般用在动词前，与动词整体做谓语，表示一种能力或者可能。其否定形式是"不能"。例如：

The verb "能" is generally used in front of the verb, as a predicate with the verb as a whole, to express a kind of ability or possibility. The negative form is "cannot", e.g.

1. 这件衣服我能试试吗？

2. 衣服能再便宜一点吗？

3. 你能和我一起去图书馆吗？

主语+不能+动词

1. 小米：再便宜一点儿吧。

   店员：对不起，不能再便宜了。

2. 明天阴天，不能去公园玩儿了。

3. 我有事情，不能和你一起去公园了。

🗨 练习 Exercises

一、听后选择正确的读音 Listen and choose the correct pronunciation

1. (　　) A. dàxiǎo　　　　B. dàxiào　　　　C. dǎxiāo

2. (　　) A. piányi　　　　B. biànyì　　　　C. piānyí

3. (　　) A. jiàgěi　　　　　B. jiàgé　　　　　C. jiāogěi

4. (　　) A. diǎnyǎ　　　　　B. huìyuán　　　　C. diànyuán

5. (　　) A. kuàilái　　　　　B. hòulái　　　　　C. hòumiàn

6. (　　) A. kāishǐ　　　　　B. kànjiàn　　　　　C. kǎnjià

二、给词语选择正确图片 Listen and choose the right picture

A.　　　　　　　　B.　　　　　　　　C.

D.　　　　　　　　E.

1. 花店(　　)　　　　2. 超市(　　)　　　　3. 食堂(　　)

4. 医院(　　)　　　　5. 服装店(　　)

三、选择所给词语的正确读音 Choose the correct pronunciation of the words given

1. (　　)花　　A. huá　　　　B. huà　　　　C. huā

2. (　　)刚　　A. kàng　　　B. gǎng　　　C. gāng

3. (　　)再见　A. zìjiàn　　　B. zàijiàn　　　C. zāijìn

4. (　　)砍价　A. kǎn jià　　B. kàn jiàn　　C. kàng jī

5. (　　)后来　A. hòulā　　　B. hòulái　　　C. xiàlái

6. (　　)看中　A. kàngzhòu　B. kànzhòng　　C. kànzhe

7. (　　)店员　A. diànyuán　B. diǎnyán　　C. diànyǐng

四、请用下列词语填空 Please fill in the blanks with the following words

A. 钱　　B. 便宜　　C. 楼下　　D. 你好　　E. 花　　F. 卖　　G. 贵

例如:我在(C)等你。

1. 可以(　　　　)一点吗?

2. 请问这件衣服多少(　　　　)?

3. 这家店是(　　　　)衣服的。

4. (　　　　),请问这件衣服怎么卖?

5. 我想买一束(　　　　)送给我的妈妈。

6. 这件衣服要比那件衣服(　　　　)一些。

五、汉字练习 Chinese character practice

1. 写出下列古代汉字对应的现代汉字 Write the modern Chinese characters corresponding to the following ancient Chinese characters

出

卖

看

2. 分析下列汉字的结构 Analyze the structure of the following Chinese characters

店　价　格　贵　宜　适

上下结构 Upper-lower structure_____

左右结构 Left-right structure_____

左上包围结构 Left-top Surrounding structure_____

左下包围结构 Lower-left Surrounding structure_____

3. 写出下列汉字的笔画 Write the strokes of the following Chinese characters

元_____

再_____

打_____

折_____

六、书写练习 Writing exercises

1. 书写汉字 Writing Chinese characters

例如：我 jiào（叫）小米。

（1）这件衣服很 héshì（　　　　）。

（2）hòulái（　　　　）我回家了。

（3）这件衣服很 piányi（　　　　）。

（4）我 kànzhòng（　　　　）这条裙子了。

（5）这双鞋子的 jiàgé（　　　　）是 100 元。

（6）我昨天去 fúzhuāngdiàn（　　　　）买衣服了。

2. 按正确的顺序组合句子并书写在横线上 Assemble the sentences in the correct order and write them on the line

例如:叫　我　大山。

　　我叫大山。

(1)衣服　请问　怎么　卖　这件

_____

(2)衣服　这件　200元　卖

_____

(3)我们　衣服　买　这件

_____

(4)超市　很　这个　大

_____

(5)小红　今天　裙子　300元　花了　买

_____

(6)这条　价格　的　裙子　100元　是

_____

(7)一起　买　服装店　去　我们　衣服　吧

_____

七、课堂活动 Class activities

两人一组,互相当顾客和店员砍价。

Working in groups of two, bargaining prices as customers and shop assistants.

第十三课　怎样支付？
Lesson 13　How to pay?

📅 **课文 Text**

课文一　Text 1

在服装店，留学生大山帮着小米砍价到450元。

At the clothing store, international student Da Shan helps Xiao Mi to cut the price to 450 RMB.

（小米拿起钱包准备付款。）

（Xiao Mi picks up her wallet and prepares to pay.）

店员：请问您怎么付款？

小米：都有哪些付款方式？

店员：微信和支付宝都可以。

小米：现金可以吗？

店员：现金不太方便。

课文二　Text 2

（小米拿起手机。）

（Xiao Mi picks up the cell phone.）

大山：小米，你有支付宝吗？

小米：有的，但是我喜欢用微信支付。

店员：如果用微信，就请扫微信码。

小米：好的。

（小米打开微信，扫码。）

（Xiao Mi opens WeChat and scans the code.）

小米：已经支付。

店员：谢谢！欢迎下次光临。

课文三　Text 3

小米买了自己喜欢的粉色裙子。在付款时，店员请她用微信或者支付宝来付款，小米用微信付款。

📝 生词 New Words

生　词	词　性	解　释	举　例
付款 fùkuǎn	vi	to pay	在哪里付款？ Where to pay？
哪些 nǎxiē	pron	which	你去过哪些国家？ Which countries have you been to？
方式 fāngshì	n	way；manner；method	支付方式有哪些？ What are the payment methods？
微信 wēixìn	n	WeChat	加个微信吧！ Add a WeChat account！
支付宝 zhīfùbǎo	n	Alipay	支付宝很方便。 Alipay is very convenient.
现金 xiànjīn	n	cash	我用现金支付。 I will pay in cash.
方便 fāngbiàn	adj	convenient；advantageous	支付宝很方便。 Alipay is very conve-nient.
用 yòng	vt	use	我能用你的电脑吗？ Can I use your computer？

续表

生 词	词 性	解 释	举 例
如果 rúguǒ	conj	if; in case; in the event of;	如果我是你，就会去。 If I were you, I would go.
扫 sǎo	vt	scan	扫文件 scan the file
微信码 wēixìnmǎ	n	WeChat QR code	你可以扫微信码支付。 You can pay by scan-ning WeChat code.
自己 zìjǐ	pron	oneself	我自己去。 I will go by myself.
或者 huòzhě	conj	or	买这个或者那个。 Buy this one or that one.
欢迎 huānyíng	v	welcome back again	欢迎下次光临。 Welcome back again.

汉 汉字 Chinese Characters

独体字(dútǐzì) Single character

方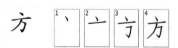

式

用

合体字(hétǐzì)　Combined character

信　左右结构 zuǒyòu jiégòu　Left-right structure　亻　言

It is an ideograph composed of 亻(人, rén, people) and 言(yán, speak). It expresses people should be honest when they talk. Therefor its primitive sense is sincerity and honesty.

扫　左右结构 zuǒyòu jiégòu　Left-right structure　扌　彐

It is an ideograph composed of 扌(手, shǒu, hands) and 彐(simplified form of 帚, zhǒu, broom). Its sense is to sweep the room with a broom in hand.

码　左右结构 zuǒyòu jiégòu　Left-right structure　石　马

It is a signific-phonetic character. Its signific element(right side) is 石(shí, stone), its phonetic element is 马(mǎ, horse). Its original meaning is agate a kind of gemstone second only to jade. It is used to express a sign or object indicating number; code.

金　上下结构 shàngxià jiégòu　Upper-lower structure　人　𡆠

It is an ideograph. The upper element 人 looks like a cover, 𡆠 means metals in soils. 金 looks like metals in soils.

款　左右结构 zuǒyòu jiégòu　Left-right structure　𡱈　欠

It is an ideograph. It is the simplified form of 欵. The left element is related to sacrifice. The right element is a man with a wide mouth in prayer. It describes the action of sincerely pray. Its primitive sense is to be sincere. Funds is its extended sense, e.g. 付款.

微   左右结构 zuǒyòu jiégòu   Left-right structure   彳 敨

It is a signific-phonetic character. Its signific element is 彳 (chì, walk slowly). Its phonetic element is 敨 (wēi, small; little; tiny). Its original meaning is to walk clandestinely. It is used to express the sense of minute; tiny; light; slight as adjective.

临   左右结构 zuǒyòu jiégòu   Left-right structure   丨 缶

0Its bronze script is 臦. Its original complex form is 臨. 临 is the modern simplified Chinese character. 𠂉 is a bent man, 臣 is wide eyes, 𠂤 is like some things. The whole character shows a person bends down and looks down at some things. Its primitive sense is to look from high to low. 光临 is a kind of honorific of presence means visitors condescend to come from high place to low place.

🗨 语法 Grammar

时间副词"已经"   The adverb of time "已经"

表示在说话前或某一特定时间前，动作状态就发生了。例如：

It means that the action state occurred before speaking or at a certain time, e.g.

教师：昨天你学汉语了吗?

学生：已经学习了。

A：那件衣服你买了吗?

B：已经买了。

A：你支付了吗?

B：已经支付了。

关联词"如果……就……"　The correlative "如果……就……"

"如果……就……"表示的是一种假设关系。假设的是一种不会发生或者不可能发生的事情。表示前分句所假定某种情况出现(或不出现)了，就会(或者也不会、也不能)引发后分句所表达的另一种情况的出现。分句之间有偏、正句之分，前偏后正。例如：

"如果……就……" represents a hypothetical relationship. What is assumed is something that will not happen or cannot happen. It means that if a certain situation assumed by the previous clause appears (or does not appear), it will (or will not, and cannot) trigger the appearance of another situation expressed by the latter clause. There is a difference between the clauses and the correct sentence, and the front is biased to the back, e.g.

1. 如果用微信，请扫码。

2. 如果明天晴天，就去公园玩儿。

3. 如果今天下雨，就在家学习汉语。

4. 如果明天是周末，我就不去上课了。

练习 Exercises

一、听后选择正确的读音 Listen and choose the correct pronunciation

1. (　　) A. nǎxiē　　　B. yòng　　　C. nín

2. (　　) A. wēixìn　　　B. wēixìng　　　C. wēixì

3. (　　) A. xiànjīng　　　B. xiànjīn　　　C. xiàngjī

4. (　　) A. fāngshì　　　B. fāngbiàn　　　C. fùkuǎn

5. (　　) A. rúguǒ　　　B. huòzhě　　　C. nǎxiē

6. (　　) A. zhīfùbǎo　　　B. wēixìnmǎ　　　C. fùkuǎnmǎ

二、给词语选择正确图片 Listen and choose the right picture

A.　　　B.　　　C.

D.　　　E.　　　F.

1. 微信（　　　）　2. 支付宝（　　　）　3. 付款码（　　　）

4. 现金（　　　）　5. 手机（　　　）　6. 扫码（　　　）

三、选择所给词语的正确读音 Choose the correct pronunciation of the words given

1. （　　　）付款　　A. fúkuān　　　B. fùkuǎn　　　C. fūkuān

2. （　　　）微信　　A. wēixìn　　　B. wéixīn　　　C. wèixīn

3. （　　　）哪些　　A. nàxiē　　　B. náxiē　　　C. nǎxiē

4. （　　　）支付宝　A. zhīfùbǎo　　B. zhǐfúbǎo　　C. zhìfùbào

5. （　　　）方便　　A. fǎngbiān　　B. fāngbiàn　　C. fàngbiān

6. （　　　）扫码　　A. sǎomǎ　　　B. sǎngmǎ　　　C. sǎomǎo

四、请用下列词语填空 Please fill in the blanks with the following words

A. 微信　　B. 付款　　C. 方便　　D. 现金　　E. 欢迎下次光临　　F. 支付宝

G. 哪些　　H. 扫　　I. 方式　　J. 如果

例如：请您慢走，（E）。

1. 请问，可以用（　　　　）吗？

2. 我觉得扫码比现金（　　　　）。

3. 我没有（　　　　），可以用支付宝吗？

4. 我们一般扫码（　　　　）。

5. 比起微信，我更喜欢用（　　　　）。

6. 你喜欢用什么（　　　　）购物？

7. （　　　　）你没现金，可以用二维码。

8. 你可以（　　　　）一下微信码。

9. （　　　　）东西在周三可以打折？

五、汉字练习 Chinese character practice

1. 找出现代汉字对应的古代汉字 Match the ancient Chinese characters and the modern

Chinese characters

临　　　　　　　ㄋ

人　　　　　　　㑇

2. 分析下列汉字的结构 Analyze the structure of the following Chinese characters

自　己　金　付　些　用　果

独体字(dútǐzì)　Single character＿＿＿＿＿＿＿＿＿＿＿＿＿＿＿＿＿＿

合体字(hétǐzì)　Combined character＿＿＿＿＿＿＿＿＿＿＿＿＿＿＿＿

3. 写出下列汉字的笔画 Write the strokes of the following Chinese characters

宝＿＿＿＿＿＿＿＿＿＿＿＿＿＿＿＿＿＿＿＿＿＿＿＿＿＿＿＿＿＿＿

信＿＿＿＿＿＿＿＿＿＿＿＿＿＿＿＿＿＿＿＿＿＿＿＿＿＿＿＿＿＿＿

用＿＿＿＿＿＿＿＿＿＿＿＿＿＿＿＿＿＿＿＿＿＿＿＿＿＿＿＿＿＿＿

扫＿＿＿＿＿＿＿＿＿＿＿＿＿＿＿＿＿＿＿＿＿＿＿＿＿＿＿＿＿＿＿

付＿＿＿＿＿＿＿＿＿＿＿＿＿＿＿＿＿＿＿＿＿＿＿＿＿＿＿＿＿＿＿

微＿＿＿＿＿＿＿＿＿＿＿＿＿＿＿＿＿＿＿＿＿＿＿＿＿＿＿＿＿＿＿

六、书写练习 Writing exercises

1. 书写汉字 Writing Chinese characters

例如：我 jiào（叫）小米。

(1)我喜欢用 wēixìn（　　　　　）买东西。

(2)可以把 fùkuǎnmǎ（　　　　　）给我吗？

(3)huānyíng xiàcì guānglín（　　　　　　　），再见！

(4)我没有 xiànjīn（　　　　　　），可以 sǎomǎ（　　　　　）吗？

(5)请问，nín（　　　　　　）是小米的父亲吗？

(6)你平常用什么 fāngshì（　　　　　　）购物呢？

2. 按正确的顺序组合句子并书写在横线上 Assemble the sentences in the correct order and write them on the line

例如：叫　我　大山

　　　我叫大山。

(1)请　付款码　扫　您

＿＿＿＿＿＿＿＿＿＿＿＿＿＿＿＿＿＿＿＿＿＿＿＿＿＿＿＿＿＿＿＿＿＿＿

（2）微信　　我　　付款　　用

_____

（3）哪些　　买　　东西　　你想

_____

（4）现金　　也　　可以　　您　　用　　付款

_____

（5）如果　　付款码　　没有　　用　　也可以　　现金　　支付

_____

（6）用　　微信　　支付宝　　和　　你　　喜欢　　吗

_____

七、课堂活动 Class activities

两人一组，一个扮演老板，一个扮演取货的人员，互相对话。

A group of two, one as the boss and the other as the pick-up staff, talk to each other.

第十四课　你会网购吗？
Lesson 14　Do you shop online?

📅 课文 Text

课文一　Text 1

在留学生公寓楼下，小米和大山刚从体育馆打完乒乓球回来，碰到急匆匆的大江。

Under the international student apartment, Xiao Mi and Da Shan have just returned from playing table tennis in the gym, and they meet Da Jiang in a hurry.

（大山和小米跟大江打招呼。）

（Da Shan and Xiao Mi greet Da Jiang.）

大山：大江，你去哪里？

大江：我去拿快递。

小米：我记得昨天你也有快递啊。

大江：是的，现在学习比较忙，没时间出去买东西。很多东西我都在网上买了。

大山：都在网上买哪些东西？

大江：水果、蔬菜、文具、衣服、化妆品，等等，都可以在网上买。很方便！

大山：是吗？水果也可以在网上买？没问题吗？

大江：没问题，又便宜又好吃。

大山：感觉很不错啊！我想试试。

课文二　Text 2

（小米听到大山和大江的对话，很高兴。）

（Hearing the conversation between Da Shan and Da Jiang, Xiao Mi is so happy.）

小米：太好了！我平时要买很多东西，尤其是水果。我也想在网上买。

大江：试试吧。

小米：怎么弄呢？你可以教教我吗？

大江：当然可以，很简单的。需要先下载京东和淘宝两个软件。

小米：这两个软件有什么不同吗？

大江：都差不多，但是京东送货最快，淘宝会慢一点。

小米：怎么下载？可以告诉我吗？

大江：没问题，等我快递取完，回来告诉你们。

小米：好的，非常感谢。

（大江取完快递，来找大山和小米。）

(After picking up the express delivery, Da Jiang came to find Da Shan and Xiao Mi.)

大江：先在软件商店下载京东和淘宝两个软件。

大山：我已经下载好了，接下来怎么办？

大江：先注册，然后登录就可以用了。

大山：好的，我试试。

小米：耶，我已经成功了！我买了苹果，好便宜啊！才 3.5 元。

大江：你真棒！

课文三　Text 3

今天，大山和小米在路上遇到大江。大江又去取快递。大江告诉大山和小米，很多东西都可以在网上买，不但便宜，而且方便。大山教他们购买的方法。大山和小米在大江的帮助下，学会了网上购物。

📝 生词 New Words

生　词	词　性	解　释	举　例
网购 wǎng gòu		online shopping	网购很方便。 Online shopping is very convenient.
取 qǔ	vt	fetch; get	取货 pick up the goods
快递 kuàidì	n	expressage	取快递 fetch express delivery

生 词	词 性	解 释	举 例
学习 xuéxí	vt	learn；study	学习新知识 learn new knowledge
比较 bǐjiào	adv	relatively；rather；fairly	我比较累。 I'm quite tired.
忙 máng	adj	busy	我现在学习比较忙。 I am currently quite busy with my studies.
网上 wǎng shàng		on the internet；on line	网上交友 make friends online
水果 shuǐguǒ	n	fruit	水果很好吃。 Fruits are delicious.
蔬菜 shūcài	n	vegetables	蔬菜很健康。 Vegetables are healthy.
化妆品 huàzhuāngpǐn	n	cosmetics	女生有很多化妆品。 Girls have a lot of cosmetics.
感觉 gǎnjué	vt	feel	我感觉很好。 I feel good.
不错 búcuò	adj	good；nice； pretty good；not bad	我感觉水果不错。 I feel the fruit is good.
真 zhēn	adv	really；truly；indeed	你真得很棒！ You are really great！
弄 nòng	vt	do	请帮我弄一下。 Please help me do it.
教 jiāo	vt	teach；instruct	你能教我网上购物吗？ Can you teach me how to shop online？
当然 dāngrán	adv	of course	我当然可以做。 Of course I can do it.
简单 jiǎndān	adj	easy；simple	这个问题很简单。 This question is easy.

生　词	词　性	解　释	举　例
下载 xiàzài	vt	download	下载软件 download the software
京东 jīngdōng	n	JDcom（Online retail platform in China）	
淘宝 táobǎo	n	Taobao（Online retail platform in China）	
软件 ruǎnjiàn	n	software	下载软件 download software
注册 zhùcè	vt	register	注册账号 register an account
登录 dēnglù	vt	login	登录网站 log in to the website
告诉 gàosù	vt	tell	让我来告诉你。 Let me tell you.
两个 liǎng gè		two	那两个人是夫妻。 Those two are husband and wife.
差不多 chàbuduō	adv	almost	两个软件差不多。 The two software are similar.
接下来 jiēxiàlái	adv	next；then	接下来要表演的是小米。 Xiaomi will perform next.
怎么办 zěnme bàn		what to do	我的钱包丢了，怎么办？ I lost my wallet. What should I do?
不但 búdàn	conj	not only；used correlatively with 而且（but also）	获奖的不但有他还有我。 Not only him but also me won the prize.
而且 érqiě	conj	but（also）；and that	这个包好看而且便宜。 This bag is beautiful and cheap.
帮助 bāngzhù	vt	help；aid；assist	我们要互相帮助。 We should help each other.

汉 汉字 Chinese Characters

独体字(dútǐzì)　Single character

网

Its oracle script is 网 . The pictographic script symbolizes the form of net.

习 | 乛 | 刁 | 习 |

Its oracle script is 习 . The pictographic script symbolizes the form offeather. Its primitive sense refers to birds practicing flying.

水 | 丿 | 小 | 水 | 水 |

Its oracle script is 水 . The pictographic script symbolizes the form of water.

果 | 丨 | 冂 | 冃 | 日 | 旦 | 早 | 果 | 果 |

Its oracle script is 果 . The pictographic script symbolizes the form of fruits on the tree.

而

合体字(hétǐzì)　Combined character

注　左右结构 zuǒyòu jiégòu　Left-right structure　氵　主

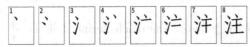

It is a signific-phonetic character. Its signific element is 氵（水，shuǐ，water），its phonetic element is 主（zhǔ，monarch）. Its original meaning is water pour into.

但　左右结构 zuǒyòu jiégòu　Left-right structure　亻旦

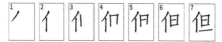

It is a signific-phonetic character. Its signific element is 亻（人，rén，people）. Its phonetic element is 旦（dàn，monarch）.

助　左右结构 zuǒyòu jiégòu　Left-right structure　且　力

It is a signific-phonetic character. Its signific element is 且（qiě，also）. Its phonetic element is 力（lì，power）.

感　上下结构 shàngxià jiégòu　Upper-lower structure　咸　心

It is an ideograph composed of 心（xīn，heart；intention）and 咸（xián，all）. Its primitive sense is to feel with heart.

蔬　上下结构 shàngxià jiégòu　Upper-lower structure　艹　疏

It is a signific-phonetic character. Its signific element is 艹（草，cǎo，grass；plant）. Its phonetic element is 疏（shū，cheap）. In ancient China, vegetables were cheaper than meat.

菜　上下结构 shàngxià jiégòu　Upper-lower structure　艹　采

It is a signific-phonetic character. Its signific element is 艹（草，cǎo，grass；plant）. Its phonetic element is 采（cǎi，pick；gather）. The oracle script of 采 is 🌿 just like picking the fruits or leaves of plants by hand. The whole character shows 菜 are edible plants picked from the garden

帮 上下结构 shàngxià jiégòu Upper-lower structure 邦 巾

It is a signific-phonetic character. Its signific element is 巾 (jīn). Its phonetic element is 邦 (bāng, nation).

载 右上包围结构 yòushàng bāowéi jiégòu Right-top surrounding structure 弌 车

It is a signific-phonetic character. Its signific element is 车 (chē, vehicle). Its phonetic element is 弌 (zāi).

🗨 语法 Grammar

能愿动词"会" The optative verb "会"

表示有能力做某事。

Indicates the ability to do something.

肯定式：会+动词+名词

Affirmative：会 + Verb + Noun

1. 我会网购。

2. 我会说汉语。

3. 他会说英语。

否定式：不会+动词+名词

Negative：不会 + Verb + Noun

1. 我不会网购。

2. 我不会说汉语。

3. 他不会说英语。

关联词"又……又……" The correlative "又……又……"

"又……又……"用来连接并列的形容词、动词或动词词组，表示两种情况或状态同时存在。例如：

"又……又……"is used to connect adjectives, verbs, or verb phrases that are side by side, indicating that two situations or states exist at the same time, e.g.

1. 公园又大又漂亮。

2. 水果又便宜又好吃。

3. 这件裙子又好又便宜。

关联词"不但……而且……" The correlative "不但……而且……"

"不但……而且……"连接一个复句，表达递进意义。"不但"用在第一个分句，常和"而且/还"等配合使用。例如：

"不但……而且……"connects a complex sentence to express progressive meaning. "而且/还" is used in the first clause, and is often used in conjunction with "and/also", e.g.

1. 他不但会网购，而且会砍价。

2. 他不但会说英语，还会说法语。

3. 网上的东西不但便宜，而且方便。

练习 Exercises

一、听后选择正确的读音 Listen and choose the correct pronunciation

1. (　　) A. wǎnggòu　　　　B. wǎngshàng　　　　C. gǎnjué

2. (　　) A. kuàidì　　　　B. dēnglù　　　　C. gàosù

3. (　　) A. jiēxiàlái　　　　B. zěnmebàn　　　　C. huàzhuāngpǐn

4. (　　) A. táobǎo　　　　B. jīngdōng　　　　C. jiǎndān

5. (　　) A. ruǎnjiàn　　　　B. shūcài　　　　C. shuǐguǒ

6. (　　) A. dāngrán　　　　B. dāngráng　　　　C. dānrán

二、给词语选择正确图片 Listen and choose the right picture

A. 　　B. 　　C.

D. 　　E. 　　F.

1. 水果(　　)　　2. 京东(　　)　　3. 淘宝(　　)

4. 蔬菜(　　)　　5. 快递(　　)　　6. 客服(　　)

三、选择所给词语的正确读音 Choose the correct pronunciation of the words given

1. (　　)淘宝　　A. táobǎo　　B. tàobāo　　C. tāobào

2. (　　)简单　　A. jiǎndān　　B. jiāndàn　　C. jiǎndàn

3. (　　)注册　　A. zhùcè　　B. zhǔchí　　C. zhǔcè

4. (　　)告诉　　A. gǎosù　　B. gàosù　　C. gāochù

5. (　　)差不多　A. chábúdao　　B. zhàbúdào　　C. chābuduō

6. (　　)网购　　A. wǎnggòu　　B. wāngōu　　C. wǎnggǎo

四、请用下列词语填空 Please fill in the blanks with the following words

A. 淘宝　　B. 网购　　C. 差不多　　D. 注册　　E. 登录　　F. 账号

G. 客服　　K. 快递

例如：你有没有(　A　)账号。

1. 首先你需要一个(　　　　　)。

2. (　　　　　)是一种很便利的方式。

3. 你可以找(　　　　　)处理。

4. 你可以帮我拿一下(　　　　　)吗？

5. 我把密码忘记了没办法(　　　　　)。

6. 我在(　　　　　)上买了一件衣服。

7. 这双鞋和那双鞋价格(　　　　　)。

五、汉字练习 Chinese character practice

1. 找出现代汉字对应的古代汉字 Match the ancient Chinese characters and the modern Chinese characters

果

水

采

2. 分析下列汉字的结构 Analyze the structure of the following Chinese characters

蔬　菜　感　觉　载　差

上下结构 Upper-lower structure _____

右上包围结构 Right-top surrounding structure _____

左上包围结构 Left-top Surrounding structure _____

3. 写出下列汉字的笔画 Write the strokes of the following Chinese characters

网_____

习_____

办_____

蔬_____

帮_____

助_____

六、书写练习 Writing exercises

1. 书写汉字 Writing Chinese characters

例如：我　jiào（叫）　小米。

（1）我可以帮你 zhùcè（　　　　　）。

（2）我要去 qǔ kuàidì（　　　　　）。

（3）我今天打算 wǎnggòu（　　　　　）。

（4）首先需要 dēnglù zhànghào（　　　　　）。

（5）你可以找 kèfú（　　　　　）帮忙。

（6）我感觉你可以先 xiàzài（　　　　　）软件。

（7）jīngdōng（　　　　　　）上的东西质量很好。

（8）我最近 xuéxí（　　　　　　）bǐjiào（　　　　　　）忙。

（9）我感觉这个 huàzhuāngpǐn（　　　　　　）很不错。

（10）你可以 gàosù（　　　　　　）我怎么 wǎnggòu（　　　　　　）吗？

2. 按正确的顺序组合句子并书写在横线上 Assemble the sentences in the correct order and write them on the line

例如：水果　淘宝　买　我在。

　　　<u>我在淘宝买水果。</u>

（1）软件　下载　首先　你

_____

（2）登录　先　然后　注册

_____

（3）怎么办　我　接下来　应该

_____

（4）苹果　网购　便宜　比较

_____

（5）差不多　价格　东西　两个

_____

（6）淘宝　便宜　比　实体店　吗

_____

七、课堂活动 Class activities

两人一组，对话网购过程。

Work in pairs to talk to the online shopping process.

第十五课　怎么取快递？
Lesson 15　How can I get the package?

📅 课文 Text

课文一　Text 1

在大江宿舍，大山和小米来请教怎么取快递。

In Da Jiang's dormitory, Da Shan and Xiao Mi come to ask how to pick up the package.

（大江端来两杯咖啡，请大山和小米坐下来谈。）

（Da Jiang brings two cups of coffee and invites Da Shan and Xiao Mi to sit down and talk.）

小米：我昨天买了苹果，可怎么去取呢？

大江：你收到手机短信了吗？如果东西到了，手机短信就会通知你到什么地方取。

小米：我没注意啊，我看看。

大江：在短信通知里。

小米：我收到了，说是到工行旁边的菜鸟驿站去取。

大江：我带你们去拿。

小米：太好了！非常感谢！

课文二　Text 2

（大江带着大山和小米来取快递。）

（Da Jiang brings Da Shan and Xiao Mi to pick up the package.）

大江：您好，我们取快递。

快递员：你手机的后四位是多少？

小米：我手机的后四位是 9737。

快递员：收货人的姓名是什么？

小米：小米。

快递员：好的，请稍等。

（快递员在一堆货物中找到小米的，递给小米。）

(The courier found Xiao Mi's delivery in a pile of goods and handed it to Xiao Mi.)

快递员：是这个吗？

小米：是的，谢谢！

（看到小米拿到快递，大江走了过来。）

(Seeing Xiao Mi get the express delivery, Da Jiang came over.)

大江：怎么样？取快递是不是很简单？

小米：真的很简单！

大江：只要告诉快递员你的手机尾号四位数和姓名，就可以了。

小米：明白了，非常感谢！

课文三　Text 3

大山和小米昨晚在大江的指点下，在网上买了水果，但是不知道怎么取。

今天两个人一起去请教大江。大江带着两个人到快递点，一起去取。

📝 生词 New Words

生　词	词　性	解　释	举　例
苹果 píngguǒ	n	apple	苹果是红色的。 Apple is red.
到 dào	prep	used as a complement to a verb to	我等到了九点。 I waited until nine o'clock.
收到 shōudào	vt	receive；get	我收到了一封信。 I received a letter.
短信 duǎnxìn	n	message	发短信 send a message

生　词	词　性	解　　释	举　　例
手机短信 shǒujī duǎnxìn	n	cell phone message	他收到手机短信。 He received a text message from his phone.
会 huì	v	be able to	我会跳舞。 I can dance.
通知 tōngzhī	n	notification	会议通知 meeting notice
地方 dìfang	n	place；space；room	武汉有很多好玩的地方。 There are many interesting places in Wuhan.
注意 zhùyì	vt	pay attention to	注意时间 pay attention to the time
看看 kànkan	vt	look；have a look	让我看看。 Let me have a look.
中国银行 Zhōngguóyínháng	n	Bank Of China	
旁边 pángbiān	n	side；adjacency	学校旁边有一家餐馆。 There is a restaurant next to the school.
菜鸟驿站 cài niǎo yìzhàn	n	communityandcampus- orientelogistics service platform	
带 dài	vt	take	带我一起玩吧！ Take me to play together!
四位 sìwèi	n	four digits	手机后四位。 The last four digits of the phone.

续表

生 词	词 性	解 释	举 例
收货人 shōuhuò rén		consignee	收货人地址 consignee's address
姓名 xìngmíng	n	name; compellation	收货人姓名 name of consignee
只要 zhǐyào	adv	so long as	只要你来了就行。 As long as you come.
快递员 kuàidìyuán	n	courier; deliveryman	快递员在送货。 The courier is delivering the goods.
手机号 shǒujī hào	n	cell-phone number	他知道快递员手机号。 He knows the courier's phone number.

汉 汉字 Chinese Characters

独体字(dútǐzì) Single character

四 | 一 |ㄇ|ㄇ|四|四

手 |一|二|三|手

Its oracle script is 𛂚. The pictographic script symbolizes the form of hand.

合体字(hétǐzì) Combined character

苹  上下结构 shàngxià jiégòu Upper-lower structure ⺿ 平

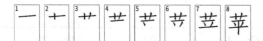

It is a signific-phonetic character. Its signific element is 艹 (草, cǎo, grass; plant). Its phonetic element is 平 (píng, flat).

意　上下结构 shàngxià jiégòu　Upper-lower structure　音　心

It is an ideograph composed of 音 (yīn, sound) and 心 (xīn, heart). Its primitive sense is words are the voice of the mind.

货　上下结构 shàngxià jiégòu　Upper-lower structure　化　贝

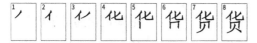

It is an ideograph composed of 化 (huà, change) and 贝 (bèi, cowry used as money in ancient times). Goods are exchanged with money.

机　左右结构 zuǒyòu jiégòu　Left-right structure　木　几

It is a signific-phonetic character. Its signific element is 木 (mù, wood). Its phonetic element is 几 (jī, a small table). Machinery was originally made of wood

银　左右结构 zuǒyòu jiégòu　Left-right structure　钅　艮

It is a signific-phonetic character. Its signific element is 钅 (金, jīn, gold; metal; money). Its phonetic element is 艮 (gèn, a small table).

递　左下包围结构 zuǒxià bāowéi jiégòu　Lower-left Surrounding structure　辶　弟

It is a signific-phonetic character. Its signific element is 辶 (chuò, walk one moment and stop the next). Its phonetic element is 弟 (dì). The oracle script of 弟 is 𢎨 like the rope is wound around the wood in a certain order. 递 means hand over, e.g. 传递; in the proper order, e.g. 递进.

📋 注释 Notes

手机号的表达 Expression of mobile phone number

手机号的位数没有地区的差别，都是 11 位，比如 13576983311 。由于手机号码位数较多，读时一般切分为"3-4-4""的停顿模式，比如 139-0107-8866 。其中号码中的"1"要读成"yāo"。例如：

There is no regional difference in the number of mobile phone numbers. They are all 11 digits, such as 13576983311. Due to the large number of digits in the mobile phone number, it is generally divided into a "3-4-4" pause mode when reading, such as 139-0107-8866. The "1" in the number should be pronounced as "yao", e.g.

18802739737 188-0273-9737

18802739838 188-0273-9838

💬 语法 Grammar

动词重叠"看看" Overlap the verb "看看"

"看看"表示动作持续的时间很短。例如：

"看看" means that the action lasts for a short time, e.g.

1. 我看看你有短信通知吗？

2. 我看看你的作业。

3. 我看看你的快递。

关联词"只要……就……" The correlative "只要……就……"

"只要"表示必要条件，"就"后面是结果。有时，结果也可以为反问句，"只要"也可以用在后一小句。例如：

"只要" indicates a necessary condition for the result that follows "就". Sometimes, the result is expressed via a rhetorical question，and "只要" can also be placed in the latter clause，e.g.

1. 只要有时间，我就上网。

2. 只要下雨，就不去公园。

3. 只要告诉快递员你的手机尾号四位数和姓名，就可以了。

练习 Exercises

一、听后选择正确的读音 Listen and choose the correct pronunciation

1. (　　) A. zhùyì　　　　B. zhǔyì　　　　C. zhùyi

2. (　　) A. píngguó　　　B. pínguǒ　　　C. pīngguǒ

3. (　　) A. duànxìng　　B. duánxìn　　　C. duǎnxìn

4. (　　) A. pángbiān　　B. bángbiān　　C. pángpian

5. (　　) A. kāngkāng　　B. kànkān　　　C. kànkan

6. (　　) A. shōudòu　　B. shōudào　　　C. shāodào

二、给词语选择正确图片 Listen and choose the right picture

A. 　　B. 　　C.

D. 　　E. 　　F.

1. 菜鸟驿站(　　)　　2. 中国银行(　　)　　3. 快递员(　　)

4. 苹果(　　)　　　5. 注意(　　)　　　6. 短信(　　)

三、给词语的正确读音 Choose the correct pronunciation of the words given

1. (　　) 姓名　　A. xìngmíng　　　B. xìnming　　　C. xìngmín

2. (　　) 只要　　A. zhíyāo　　　　B. zhǐyòu　　　C. zhǐyào

3. (　　) 短信　　A. dǎnxìn　　　　B. duǎnxìn　　　C. duànxìn

4. (　　)苹果　　A. píngguo　　　　B. pínggǒ　　　　C. píngguǒ

5. (　　)旁边　　A. pángbiān　　　B. pángbān　　　C. bángbiān

6. (　　)收货人　A. shōhuò rèn　　B. shōuhuò rèn　　C. shōuhuò rén

四、请用下列词语填空 Please fill in the blanks with the following words

A. 收到　　B. 菜鸟驿站　　C. 收货人　　D. 快递员　　E. 地方

F. 通知　　G. 旁边

例如：你(A)手机短信了吗？

1. (　　　　)的姓名是什么？

2. 我(　　　　)你们去拿。

3. 短信通知到工行旁边的(　　　　)去取。

4. 我收到了，说是到工行(　　　　)的菜鸟驿站去取。

5. 如果东西到了，会有手机短信通知你到什么(　　　　)取。

6. 只要告诉(　　　　)你的手机尾号四位数和你的姓名就可以了。

五、汉字练习 Chinese character practice

1. 找出现代汉字对应的古代汉字 Match the ancient Chinese characters and the modern Chinese characters

意

鸟

手

2. 分析下列汉字的结构 Analyze the structure of the following Chinese characters

边　驿　递　站　机　短　国

左下包围结构 Lower-left surrounding structure＿＿＿＿＿＿＿＿＿＿

左右结构 Left-right structure ＿＿＿＿＿＿＿＿＿＿

全包围结构 Whole-surround structure ＿＿＿＿＿＿＿＿＿＿

3. 写出下列汉字的笔画。Write the strokes of the following Chinese characters

短＿＿＿＿＿＿＿＿＿＿

信＿＿＿＿＿＿＿＿＿＿

快＿＿＿＿＿＿＿＿＿＿

递＿＿＿＿＿＿＿＿＿＿

六、书写练习 Writing exercises

1. 书写汉字 Writing Chinese characters

例如：我 jiào（叫）小米。

（1）我没注意啊，我 kànkan（   ）啊。

（2）在 duǎnxìn tōngzhī（   ）里。

（3）大江 dài（   ）着大山和小米来取快递。

（4）你收到 shǒujī duǎnxìn（   ）了吗？

（5）我昨天买了 píngguǒ（   ），可怎么去取呢？

2. 按正确的顺序组合句子并书写在横线上 Assemble the sentences in the correct order and write them on the line

例如：多少　　是　　手机　　的　　你　　后　　四位

　　　你手机的后四位是多少？

（1）昨天　　苹果　　买　　我　　了

_____

（2）里　　通知　　在　　短信

_____

（3）收到　　了　　我

_____

（4）什么　　的　　是　　收货人　　姓名

_____

（5）短信　　了　　你　　吗　　收到

_____

七、课堂活动 Class activities

两人一组，扮演快递员与取货人进行取快递对话。

As a group of two, act as a courier and have a conversation with the picker.

第十六课 为什么没来上课？
Lesson 16　Why aren't you in class?

📅 课文 Text

课文一　Text 1

在教室，今天是王老师的综合汉语课，同学们都早早地来到了教室。

In the classroom, today is Teacher Wang's Integrated Chinese class, and the students all come to the classroom early.

（上课铃响了，王老师点名。）

(The bell rings, and Teacher Wang calls names.)

王老师：大山。

小米：王老师，大山没来。

王老师：大山，还在睡觉吗？

小米：他已经起床了，现在正在吃早饭，马上来。

课文二　Text 2

（第二节课下课了，大山还没来，王老师走到小米身旁。）

(The second class is over and Da Shan has not yet arrived, Teacher Wang walks to Xiao Mi's side.)

王老师：小米，大山还没来？

小米：是的。

王老师：他今天还上课吗？

小米：不知道。

大卫：大山出去玩儿了吧。

阿力：我想，他可能还在睡觉。

安娜：他是不是生病了？

（第二节课铃声响了，大家都坐好，准备上课，这时大山走了进来。）

(The bell rings for the second class, everyone seats and is ready for the class, Da Shan walks in.)

王老师：大山你迟到了。

大山：王老师，对不起。

王老师：为什么迟到？

大山：我起床后，头很痛，去医院看医生了。

王老师：现在好点儿了吗？

大山：好点儿了。

王老师：下次一定要请假。

大山：好的，我知道了。谢谢王老师！

课文三 Text 3

今天，综合汉语课，大山因去医院看病，迟到了一节课，王老师告诉他，下次一定要请假。

📝 生词 New Words

生 词	词 性	解 释	举 例
睡觉 shuìjiào	vi	sleep	我晚上十点睡觉。 I go to sleep at ten o'clock in the evening.
起床 qǐ chuáng		rise; get up; get out of bed	起床了！ It's time to get up.
正在 zhèngzài	adv	be being; in process of	他正在睡觉，还没起床。 He is sleeping and hasn't gotten up yet.
早饭 zǎofàn	n	breakfast	吃早饭 eat breakfast

续表

生 词	词 性	解 释	举 例
马上 mǎshàng	adv	immediately；right away；at once	我马上到。 I will be there right away.
上课 shàngkè	vi	attend class；go to class；give a class	我要去上课。 I'm going to class.
出去 chūqù	vi	go out；get out：	出去玩 go out for fun
可能 kěnéng	adv	maybe；perhaps；possibly	可能他忘记了。 Maybe he forget it.
生病 shēngbìng	vi	be taken ill	我生病了。 I'm sick.
迟到 chídào	adj	be late	他迟到可能是因为生病了。 He may be late because he's sick.
头 tóu	n	head	他的头很大。 He has a big head.
痛 tòng	n	pain；grief；anguish；sadness	肚子痛 stomach pain
医院 yīyuàn	n	hospital	医院就在附近。 The hospital is nearby.
医生 yīshēng	n	doctor	医生让我吃药。 The doctor asked me to take medicine.
看医生 kàn yīshēng		see a doctor	她头痛去医院看医生了。 She went to the hospital to see a doctor for a headache.
下次 xiàcì	adv	next time	下次见! See you next time!

生　词	词　性	解　释	举　例
一定 yídìng	adv	certainly	你一定会成功的。 You will definitely succeed.
要 yào	vt	will; shall; be about to; be going to	我要去上学。 I'm going to school.
请假 qǐngjià	vi	ask for leave; beg off	下次你一定要请假。 You must ask for leave next time.

汉字 Chinese Characters

独体字(dútǐzì)　Single character

马　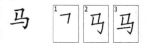

Its oracle script is 🐎. The pictographic script symbolizes the form of horse.

生　丿　𠂉　牛　生

Its oracle script is ↓. The pictographic script symbolizes a bud grows on the ground. Its primitive sense is to grow.

合体字(hétǐzì)　Combined character

去　上下结构 shàngxià jiégòu　Upper-lower structure　土　厶

Its oracle script is 𠔉. Upper element is a person. Lower element is a cave.

The pictographic script symbolizes a man is leaving the cave.

早 　上下结构 shàngxià jiégòu　Upper-lower structure　日　十

睡 　左右结构 zuǒyòu jiégòu　Left-right structure　目　垂

It is a signific-phonetic character. Its signific element is 目（mù, eye）. The Chinese characters with this radical are all related to eyes, e.g. 看；眼睛. The phonetic element is 垂（chuí, hang down; droop; let fall）. The original meaning refers to drooping eyelids and dozing off.

院 　左右结构 zuǒyòu jiégòu　Left-right structure　阝　完

It is a signific-phonetic character. Its signific element is 阜（fù, mound）. The Chinese characters with this radical are all related to terrain, e.g. 阴（North of the mountain）；阳（south of the mountain）；院（courtyard）. The phonetic element is 完（wán, complete）.

迟 　左下包围结构 zuǒxià bāowéi jiégòu　Lower-left Surrounding structure　辶　尺

It is a signific-phonetic character. Its signific element is 辶（chuò, stop and go）. The Chinese characters with this radical are all related to walk, e.g. 进（move forward）；退（move back）. The phonetic element is 尺（chǐ, Chinese measure approx, foot）

床 　左上包围结构 zuǒshàng bāowéi jiégòu　Left-top Surrounding structure　广　木

Its ancient Chinese character writing is 牀. It is a signific-phonetic character. The signific element is 木(mù, wood). The phonetic element is 爿(chuáng, bed). 床 is another form of writing.

痛　左上包围结构 zuǒshàng bāowéi jiégòu　Left-top Surrounding structure　疒　甬

It is a signific-phonetic character. Its signific element is 疒(jí, sick). The phonetic element is 甬(yǒng). In this character 甬 is the abbreviated form of 通(tōng, open; through). Pain leads to obstruction.

医　左三包围结构 zuǒsān bāowéi jiégòu　Top-left-bottom surrounding structure　匚　矢

It is a signific-phonetic character. Its signific element is 匚(fāng, container). The phonetic element is 矢(shǐ, arrow). The pronunciation of 矢 and 医 is similar in ancient Chinese. But the pronunciation is different in modern Chinese.

语法 Grammar

固定格式"是不是"　The fixed expression "是不是"

提问人对某个事实或者情况有比较肯定的估计，为了进一步得到证实，而用"是不是"来提问。"是不是"用在谓语前面：主语+是不是+谓语？例如：

The questioner has a more positive estimate of a certain fact or situation, and in order to be further confirmed, "是不是" is often used to ask the question. "是不是" is used in front of the predicate：Subject + is it + Predicate？E.g.

1. 他是不是生病了？
2. 他是不是还在睡觉？
3. 他是不是不来上课了？

助动词"要"　The auxiliary verb "要"

用在动词前，表示有做某件事情的意愿。例如：

"要"is used before a verb to indicate a willingness to do something，e.g.

主语 + 要

Subject + 要

王老师：下次一定要请假。

大山：好的，我知道了。谢谢王老师！

王老师：大山要来上课吗？

小米：要来上课。

A：你要取什么？

B：我要取快递。

练习 Exercises

一、听后选择正确的读音 Listen and choose the correct pronunciation

1. (   ) A. shuìqiào   B. shuìjiào   C. shuìjào

2. (   ) A. qǐchuǎng   B. qǐchuáng   C. qíchuáng

3. (   ) A. zǎofàn   B. zǎfàn   C. zǎofàng

4. (   ) A. mǎshàng   B. máshàng   C. mǎshǎng

5. (   ) A. shànggè   B. shǎngkè   C. shàngkè

6. (   ) A. chūjù   B. chūqu   C. chūqù

二、给词语选择正确图片 Listen and choose the right picture

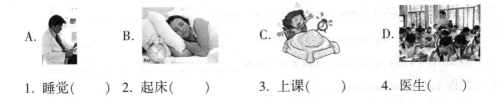

A.   B.   C.   D.

1. 睡觉(   )   2. 起床(   )   3. 上课(   )   4. 医生(   )

三、选择所给词语的正确读音 Choose the correct pronunciation of the words given

1. (   ) 正在   A. zhèngzà   B. zhèngzài   C. zhènzài

2. (   ) 出去   A. chūqù   B. chūqù   C. chūjù

3. (   ) 请假   A. qíngjià   B. qǐngjià   C. qǐngqià

4. (   ) 睡觉   A. shuìqiào   B. suìjiào   C. shuìjiào

5. (　　)马上　　A. máshàng　　　B. mǎshàng　　　C. mǎsháng

6. (　　)生病　　A. shēnbìn　　　B. shēngbìng　　　C. shēngpìn

四、请用下列词语填空 Please fill in the blanks with the following words

A. 请假　　B. 马上　　C. 生病　　D. 上课　　E. 可能　　F. 睡觉　　G. 要

例如：下次一定要(A)。

1. 他是不是(　　　　)了？

2. 大山，还在(　　　　)吗？

3. 他今天还(　　　　)吗？

4. 我想，他(　　　　)还在睡觉。

5. 下次一定(　　　　)请假。

6. 他已经起床了，现在正在吃早饭，(　　　　　　)来。

五、汉字练习 Chinese character practice

1. 找出现代汉字对应的古代汉字 Match the ancient Chinese characters and the modern Chinese characters

去

生

马

2. 分析下列汉字的结构 Analyze the structure of the following Chinese characters

起　　到　　迟　　痛　　医　　床　　课

左三包围结构 Top-left-bottom surrounding structure _____

左上包围结构 Left-top surrounding structure _____

左下包围结构 Lower-left surrounding structure _____

左右结构 Left-right structure _____

3. 写出下列汉字的笔画 Write the strokes of the following Chinese characters

早 _____

睡 _____

饭 _____

出 _____

院 _____

六、书写练习 Writing exercises

1. 书写汉字 Writing Chinese characters

例如：我 jiào（叫）小米。

（1）为什么 chídào（　　　　　）?

（2）下次 yídìng（　　　　　）要请假

（3）大家 chūqù（　　　　　）玩儿了吧。

（4）我想，他 kěnéng（　　　　　）还在睡觉。

（5）大山，还在 shuìjiào（　　　　　）吗？

（6）我起床后，头很 tòng（　　　　　），去看医生了。

2. 按正确的顺序组合句子并书写在横线上 Assemble the sentences in the correct order and write them on the line

例如：是不是　他　了　生病

　　　他是不是生病了？

（1）正在　早饭　现在　吃

_____

（2）你　了　大山　迟到

_____

（3）已经　他　起床　了

_____

（4）请假　一定　下次　要

_____

（5）还　今天　他　上课　吗

_____

（6）可能　睡觉　还　他　在

_____

（7）早早地　教室　来到　同学们　了　都

_____

七、课堂活动 Class activities

两人一组，分别扮演老师和同学，询问未来上课的原因。

Work in pairs, play the role of teacher and classmates, and ask about the reason for the absence from the class.

171

第十七课 学了多长时间汉语？

Lesson 17 How long have you been learning Chinese?

📅 **课文 Text**

课文一 Text 1

在教室，下课休息时间，王老师和大家聊天。

In the classroom, during the break after class, Teacher Wang chats with everyone.

（小米在喝咖啡，王老师走过来。）

(Xiao Mi is drinking coffee and Teacher Wang approaches.)

王老师：小米，你在你的国家学习过汉语吗？

小米：学习过。

王老师：学了多长时间？

小米：学了三个月。

王老师：你觉得汉语难吗？

小米：老师，我觉得汉语不难，我非常喜欢学习。

王老师：真棒！

课文二 Text 2

（安娜从洗手间回来，看到王老师和小米聊天，也走了过来。）

(Anna comes back from the bathroom, seeing Teacher Wang and Xiaomi talking and she comes over and joins their conversation as well.)

王老师：安娜原来学过汉语吗？

安娜：没有学过。

王老师：一点儿都没学过吗?

安娜：没有。来中国的时候，我只会说"你好""谢谢""再见"。

王老师：你觉得汉语难吗?

安娜：老师，我觉得汉语很难，尤其是汉字，我一点儿都不会写。

王老师：没关系，慢慢学吧。

课文三 Text 3

小米来中国前，在自己的国家学习了三个月汉语，她很喜欢汉语，觉得汉语一点儿也不难。

安娜来中国前，一点儿汉语也没学，只会说"你好""谢谢""再见"，她觉得汉语很难，尤其是汉字，她觉得更难。

📝 生词 New Words

生 词	词 性	解 释	举 例
国家 guójiā	n	state; nation; country; nationality	你来自哪个国家? Which country are you come from?
汉语 hànyǔ	n	Chinese	说汉语 speak Chinese
学 xué	vt	learn	我在学画画。 I'm learning to draw.
过 guò	dynamic auxiliary word	used after a verb to indicate the completion of an action.	你去过北京吗? Have you ever been to Beijing?
学过 xué guò		have learned	我学过跳舞。 I have learned to dance.
多长 duō cháng		how long	这条路有多长? How long is this road?
时间 shíjiān	n	time	你学过多长时间汉语? How long have you studied Chinese?

续表

生 词	词 性	解 释	举 例
月 yuè	n	month；the moon	一年有十二个月。 There are twelve months in a year.
三个月 sān gè yuè		three months	这个小孩三个月了。 This child is three months old.
觉得 juéde	vt	think	你觉得怎么样？ What do you think？
难 nán	adj	difficult；hard	我觉得汉语难。 I think Chinese is difficult.
容易 róngyì	adj	easy；likely	开车很容易。 It's easy to drive.
真棒 zhēnbàng		awesome；great；excellent	你真棒！ You are awesome！
原来 yuánlái	adj	former；original	原来我很害羞。 I used to be shy.
只 zhǐ	adv	only；merely	只有你能做到。 Only you can do it.
再见 zàijiàn	vi	good-bye	
发音 fāyīn	vi	pronounce	这个词怎么发音？ How to pronounce this word？
读 dú	vt	read	读书 read books
写 xiě	vt	write	写汉字 write Chinese characters
前 qián	prep	before	
一点儿都不 yī diǎnr dōu bù		not at all	汉语一点儿都不难。 Chinese is not difficult at all.

 汉字 Chinese Characters

独体字(dútǐzì)　Single character

三

月

Its oracle script is 𝕯 , it is a pictograph character and it looks like the shape of the crescent moon. Its primitive sense is the moon.

再

合体字(hétǐzì)　Combined character

棒　左右结构 zuǒyòu jiégòu　Left-right structure　木　奉

It is a signific-phonetic character. Its signific element is 木(mù, wood). Its phonetic element is 奉(fèng, carry). The pronunciation of 奉 and 棒 is the same in ancient Chinese. its primitive sense is wooden staff. Its extended sense is strong; excellent; good, e.g. 真棒.

写　上下结构 shàngxià jiégòu　Upper-lower structure　冖　与

Its traditional character is 寫. It is a signific-phonetic character. The signific element is 宀(mián, roof). Its phonetic element is 舄(xì). 写 is the simplified Chinese character.

前 上下结构 shàngxià jiégòu Upper-lower structure ⸺ 刖

Its bronze script is 𣥃. The ideograph is composed of two elements：one element is 屮 (zhǐ, foot；go forward), and the other element is (舟, zhōu, boat). It means a ship moves forward. 前 is the modern simplified Chinese character.

易 上下结构 shàngxià jiégòu Upper-lower structure 日 勿

易 was originally written as 𤲬 like a lizard. Its primitive sense is lizard. Easy is its extended sense, e.g. 容易.

原 左上包围结构 zuǒshàng bāowéi jiégòu Left-top Surrounding structure 厂 泉

Its bronze script is 𠪥. The ideograph is composed of two elements：one element is 厂 (hǎn, cliff cave), and the other element is 𤽄 (泉, quán, spring). It means a spring gushing out of the cliff. Therefor its primitive sense is waterhead. One of its extended senses is original, e. g. 原来 (original).

间 上三包围结构 shàngsān bāowéi jiégòu Left-top-right surrounding structure 门 日

Its bronze script is 𨳆. The ideograph is composed of two elements：one element is a door 門(门), and the other element is the 𝄇 (月, the moon). It means to see the moon through the gap between the two doors. Therefor its primitive sense is gap. 𝄇 was later written as 日.

📋 注释 Notes

月份　Month

月　份	拼　音	英　文
1 月	yīyuè	January
2 月	èryuè	February
3 月	sānyuè	March
4 月	sìyuè	April
5 月	wǔyuè	May
6 月	liùyuè	June
7 月	qīyuè	July
8 月	bāyuè	August
9 月	jiǔyuè	September
10 月	shíyuè	October
11 月	shíyīyuè	November
12 月	shíèryuè	December
几月	jǐ yuè	Which month

💬 语法 Grammar

动态助词"过"　The dynamic particle "过"

动态助词"过"，表示曾经发生某一动作或存在某一状态，但现在已经不再进行，这种状态已经结束。

The dynamic particle "过" means that a certain action has occurred or a certain state exists, but it is no longer carried out now, and this state has ended.

主语 + 动词 + 过 + 宾语

Subject + Verb + 过 + Object

1. A：你在你的国家学习过汉语吗？

   B：学习过。

2. A：你去过王老师家吗？

   B：去过。

3. A：你看过中国电影吗？

   B：没看过。

固定格式"……的时候" The fixed expression "……的时候"

"……的时候"是一种结构比较复杂的时间状语，多用在主语之前，用来表示事情发生的时间。事情发生的时间。例如：

"……的时候" is a time adverbial with a complex structure, which is often used before the subject to indicate the time when something happened. The time it happened，e.g.

1. 来中国的时候，我只会说"你好""谢谢""再见"。

2. 昨天晚上九点的时候，你在做什么？

3. 上课的时候，我们要写汉字。

练习 Exercises

一、请听下面的词语，选择对应的拼音 Listen and choose the correct pronunciation

1. (　　) A. shíjiān　　　B. síjiān　　　C. shíjiā　　　D. zhíjiā

2. (　　) A. guójiā　　　B. zuójiā　　　C. guóqiā　　　D. kuójiā

3. (　　) A. zàijiàn　　　B. zhàijiàn　　　C. kànjiàn　　　D. zàiqiàn

4. (　　) A. hàyǔ　　　B. hànyǔ　　　C. gànyǔ　　　D. lànyǔ

5. (　　) A. róngyì　　　B. róuyì　　　C. lóngyì　　　D. róngzì

6. (　　) A. luánlái　　　B. yuánlá　　　C. yánlái　　　D. yuánlái

二、听后选择正确的图片 Listen and choose the right picture

A.　　　　　　　B. 壹月　　　　C.

1. 一月（　　）　　2. 一个月（　　）　　3. 一个月亮（　　）

三、选择所给词语的正确读音 Choose the correct pronunciation of the words given

1. (　　) 汉语　　A. hànyǔ　　　B. gànyǔ　　　C. hàyǔ　　　D. hàuyǔ

2. (　　) 容易　　A. lóngyì　　　B. róngyì　　　C. róngqì　　　D. hóngyì

3. (　　) 原来　　A. yuánlái　　B. luánlái　　C. yuánhái　　D. yuánlá

4. (　　) 国家　　A. guójiā　　　B. luójiā　　　C. guóqiā　　　D. guóji

5. (　　) 学　　　A. qué　　　　B. xué　　　　C. xié　　　　D. jué

6. (　　) 写　　　A. xiě　　　　B. qiě　　　　C. xuě　　　　D. jiě

四、请用下列词语填空 Please fill in the blanks with the following words

A. 一月　　B. 一个月　　C. 一个月亮　　D. 一个月了

1. 我来中国（　　　　）。

2. 元旦节在（　　　　）。

3. 今晚，我看见了（　　　　）。

4. 我学汉语用了（　　　　）时间

5. 一年中，我最喜欢（　　　　）。

6. 给你（　　　　）的时间写完这篇文章

五、汉字练习 Chinese character practice

1. 找出现代汉字对应的古代汉字 Match the ancient Chinese characters and the modern Chinese characters

前　　　　　　　　火

来　　　　　　　　弓

易　　　　　　　　貝

2. 分析下列汉字的结构 Analyze the structure of the following Chinese characters

时 棒 原 过

左下包围结构 Lower-left Surrounding structure_____

左右结构 Left-right structure_____

左上包围结构 Left-top surrounding structure_____

3. 写出下列汉字的笔画 Write the strokes of the following Chinese characters

容_____

读_____

写_____

难_____

觉_____

得_____

六、书写练习 Writing exercises

1. 按正确的顺序组合句子并书写在横线上 Assemble the sentences in the correct order and write them on the line

(1)汉语　学过　我

_____

(2)我　汉语　认为　不难

_____

(3)学过　一个月　我　汉语

_____

(4)中国　来　一个　月了　小明

_____

(5)我　汉语　一个　月了　学

_____

(6)汉语　喜欢　学习　我

_____

2. 书写汉字 Writing Chinese characters

(1)我 xué(　　　　)过汉语。

(2)我认为汉语很 róngyì(　　　　)。

(3)你 zhēnbàng(　　　　)。

(4)我 juéde(　　　　)汉语很难。

（5）我学过 hànyǔ（　　　　　）。

（6）你来中国 duō cháng（　　　　　）时间了？

七、课堂活动 Class activities

两人一组，分别扮演老师和同学，互相询问对于汉语学习的看法。

In groups of two, play the role of teacher and classmate respectively, and ask each other their views on Chinese language learning.

第十八课　你汉语说得怎么样？
Lesson 18　How is your spoken Chinese?

📅 课文 Text

课文一　Text 1

在留学生公寓，一天，小米的邻居刚来中国的伊朗女孩海门来找小米。

In the student dormitory, one day, Xiao Mi's neighbor, Haimen, an Iranian girl who has just arrived in China, comes to see Xiao Mi.

（小米听到敲门声，过来开门。）

（Xiao Mi hears the knock on the door and comes to open it.）

海门：你好，请问你汉语说得怎么样？

小米：还行，怎么了？

海门：我感冒了，想去校医院看病，但不会汉语，你能陪我一起去吗？

小米：可以，没问题。

海门：非常感谢。

小米：不客气。

课文二　Text 2

（在校医院，医生在给海门看病。）

（In the school hospital, the doctor is treating Haimen.）

医生：你好，请问哪里不舒服？

小米：她感冒了，头很疼。

医生：高烧吗？

小米：有点儿热。

医生：喉咙痛吗?

小米：有点儿痛。

医生：请量一下体温。

（护士给海门量体温。）

(The nurse took Haimen's temperature.)

医生：37.5度，体温不太高，吃点药吧，然后回去多喝点水，注意休息。

小米：好的。谢谢!

医生：不客气，再见!

小米：再见。

课文三 Text 3

刚来中国不久的伊朗留学生海门，因感冒想去医院看病。但是因不懂汉语，自己不敢去。于是找到邻居小米，问小米汉语怎么样? 可以陪自己去医院吗? 小米同意了，陪着海门去校医院看病。

✐ 生词 New Words

生 词	词 性	解 释	举 例
得 de	prep	used after verbs and adjectives to express results or traits	他跑得快。 He runs fast.
还行 háixíng	adj	not bad；pretty good	我汉语说得还行。 I speak Chinese well.
感冒 gǎnmào	vi	catch a cold；have a cold	我感冒了。 I catch a cold.
看病 kàn bìng	vi	go to hospital	你需要去看病。 You need to go to hospital.
陪 péi	vt	accompany	我会陪你。 I will accompany you.

续表

生 词	词 性	解 释	举 例
没问题 méi wèn tí		no problem	
感谢 gǎnxiè	vt	thank	感谢你。 Thank you.
非常感谢 fēicháng gǎnxiè		thank you very much	非常感谢你！ Thank you very much！
不客气 bú kèqi		you're welcome	
舒服 shūfu	adj	comfortable	被子很舒服。 The quilt is very comfortable.
疼 téng	vi	ache	头疼 headache
高烧 gāoshāo	n	high fever	发高烧 have a high fever
试一下 shì yíxià		have a try；want a go	我想试一下。 I want to have a try.
体温 tǐwēn	n	body temperature	体温正常。 The body temperature is normal.
喉咙 hóulóng	n	throat；throttle	喉咙疼 sore throat
度 dù	quant	degree（a classifier for temperature）	气温多少度？ What's the temperature？
高 gāo	adj	tall；high	大树很高。 The tree is tall.
药 yào	n	medicine	吃药 take the medicine
点儿 diǎnr	adj	a bit；a little	有点儿累 a little tired
回去 huíqù	vt	return；go back	回去休息。 Go back to rest.

续表

生 词	词 性	解 释	举 例
喝 hē	vt	drink	你想喝什么? What would you like to drink?
水 shuǐ	n	water	喝点儿水 drink some water
休息 xiūxi	vi	have a rest; take a rest	你需要休息。 You need to rest.
留学生 liúxuéshēng	n	student abroad	我是留学生。 I am an international student.
懂 dǒng	vt	understand; know	你听懂了吗? Do you understand?
敢 gǎn	vt	dare	我敢潜水。 I dare to dive.

汉字 Chinese Characters

独体字(dútǐzì) Single character

儿 | ﾉ | 儿

Its oracle script is 𦥑. The pictographic script symbolizes the form of a big head baby.
Its primitive sense is baby.

非 | 丨 | 刂 | 刲 | 刲 | 非 | 非 | 非 | 非

高 | 丶 | 亠 | 广 | 亠 | 亠 | 户 | 高 | 高 | 高 | 高

Its oracle script is 高 like a tall building.

合体字(hétǐzì)　Combined character

休　左右结构 zuǒyòu jiégòu　Left-right structure　亻　木

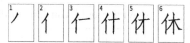

It is an Ideograph composed of two elements：left element is a person 亻(人), right element is a tree 木. A person rests by a tree. Its primitive sense is being at rest, e. g. 休息(take a rest).

试　左右结构 zuǒyòu jiégòu　Left-right structure　讠　式

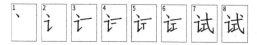

It is a signific-phonetic character. The signific element is 讠(yán, speech; word). Its phonetic element is 式(shì, type; style; pattern; form).

药　上下结构 shàngxià jiégòu　Upper-lower structure　艹　约

Its traditional character is 藥. It is a signific-phonetic character. And it is an Ideograph too. The signific element is 艹(cǎo, grass). Its phonetic element is 樂(乐 lè/yào/yuè, happy; like). 药 is the modern simplified Chinese character.

喝　左右结构 zuǒyòu jiégòu　Left-right structure　口　曷

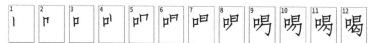

It is a signific-phonetic character. Its signific element is 口(kǒu, mouth), its phonetic element is 曷(hé).

敢　左右结构 zuǒyòu jiégòu　Left-right structure　耳　攵

Its bronze script is 𩰊. The upper element is a beast 𤝗, and the lower right element is a hand 𠂇, the two elements describe a hand grabbing beast to express the sense of brave. And the lower left element is its phonetic element 𠙵（甘，gān）. It is a signific-phonetic character.

懂　左右结构 zuǒyòu jiégòu　Left-right structure　忄　董

It is a signific-phonetic character. Its signific element is 忄（xīn, heart; mind; feeling）, its phonetic element is 董（dǒng）.

语法 Grammar

副词"还"　The adverb "还"

表示程度比较轻、勉强过得去。例如：

"还" indicates that the degree is relatively light and barely passable, e.g.

海门：你好，请问你汉语说得怎么样？

小米：还行，怎么了？

A：你汉字写得好吗？

B：还可以。

状态补语 Status complement

状态补语主要指动词后用"得"连接的表示动作结果、状态的补语。状态补语主要是对动作进行描写、评价或判断，大多由形容词或形容词短语充当，一般在形容词前要加"很"。例如：

Complement of state mainly refers to the complement of result and state of the actions which is connected with "得" after the verb. State complements are mainly used to describe, evaluate or judge actions. Most of them are used as adjectives or adjective phrases. Generally, "很" is added before the adjective. e.g.

主语 + 动词 + 得 + 形容词

Subject + Verb + 得 + Adj

A：小米汉语说得好吗？

B：小米汉语说得很好。

A：大卫汉字写得好吗？

B：大卫汉字写得很好。

A：他跑得快吗？

B：他跑得很快。

动词 + 一下　Verb + "一下"

动词 + "一下"表示一次短暂的动作。例如：

Verb + "一下" means a short action，e.g.

1. 下课了，我们可以休息一下。

2. 这条裙子很漂亮，我想试一下。

3. 这本书很有名，我想看一下。

🔊 练习 Exercises

一、请听下面的词语选择对应的拼音 Listen and choose the correct pronunciation

1. (　　) A. gǎnmào　　　　B. gǎmào　　　　C. gǎnmiào　　　　D. lǎnmào

2. (　　) A. yīluàn　　　　B. yīyuàn　　　　C. yīquàn　　　　D. līyuàn

3. (　　) A. gǎnxiè　　　　B. gǎxiè　　　　C. gǎnxè　　　　D. hǎnxiè

4. (　　) A. shūfu　　　　B. sūfu　　　　C. shūfa　　　　D. chūfu

5. (　　) A. gāosāo　　　　B. gāoshāo　　　　C. gāshāo　　　　D. lāoshāo

6. (　　) A. hóulón　　　　B. hólóng　　　　C. kóulóng　　　　D. hóulóng

二、听后选择正确的词 Listen and choose the right word

1. 医院　　2. 学校　　3. 邮局　　4. 食堂　　5. 购物中心

三、选择所给词语的正确读音 Choose the correct pronunciation of the words given

1. 看病(　　)　A. kànbìng　　B. lànbìng　　C. kànbìn　　D. kàibìng

2. 喉咙(　　)　A. hóulóng　　B. kóulóng　　C. hóukóng　　D. hóulón

3. 医院(　　) 　A. yīyuàn 　　B. yīluàn 　　C. yīquàn 　　D. līyuàn

4. 感谢(　　) 　A. gǎxiè 　　B. gǎnxiè 　　C. gǎnxè 　　D. hǎnxiè

5. 舒服(　　) 　A. sūfu 　　B. shūfa 　　C. shūfu 　　D. sūhu

6. 体温(　　) 　A. tǐwēng 　　B. tǐwēn 　　C. qǐwēn 　　D. tǐkēn

四、请用下列词语填空 Please fill in the blanks with the following words

A. 得　　B. 能　　C. 一起　　D. 陪　　E. 敢

1. 你发烧了，你(　　　　)去医院。

2. 我和你(　　　　)去上学。

3. 我(　　　　)用下你的笔吗？

4. 别怕！我(　　　　)你一起去。

5. 你(　　　　)多吃水果和蔬菜。

五、汉字练习 Chinese character practice

1. 找出现代汉字对应的古代汉字 Match the ancient Chinese characters and the modern Chinese characters

敢　　　　　　合

高　　　　　　休

休　　　　　　高

2. 分析下列汉字的结构 Analyze the structure of the following Chinese characters

疼　看　院　谢　得　病　感　冒

左右结构 Left-right structure _____

左上包围结构 Left-top surrounding structure _____

上下结构 Upper-lower structure _____

3. 写出下列汉字的笔画 Write the strokes of the following Chinese characters

非 _____

常 _____

感 _____

谢 _____

高 _____

烧 _____

六、书写练习 Writing exercises

1. 按正确的顺序组合句子并书写在横线上 Assemble the sentences in the correct order and write them on the line

(1) 休息　你　回去　要　后　好好

_____

(2) 去　得　你　医院

_____

(3) 疼　你的　喉咙　吗

_____

(4) 体温　你的　高　有点

_____

(5) 了　你　感冒

_____

(6) 体温　量一下　请

_____

2. 书写汉字 Writing Chinese characters

(1) 我的喉咙 téng(　　　　　)。

(2) 你的 tǐwēn(　　　　　)有点高。

(3) 你 gǎnmào(　　　　　)了。

(4) 你的体温有点 gāo(　　　　　)。

(5) 生病了就得吃 yào(　　　　　)。

(6) 我陪你去 yīyuàn(　　　　　)。

七、课堂活动 Class activities

两人一组，分别扮演医生和同学进行会话。

In groups of two, play the role of a doctor and have a conversation with a classmate.

第十九课 考试难不难？
Lesson 19　Is the exam difficult?

📅 **课文 Text**

课文一　Text 1

在教室，学生向王老师询问有关期末考试的事情。

In the classroom, students ask Teacher Wang about their final exams.

（下课铃声响了，王老师正准备离开。）

(The bell rings and Teacher Wang is about to leave.)

大山：老师，我们什么时候考试？

王老师：下星期二考试。

大卫：在哪个教室考？

王老师：在217。

安娜：考读写还是听说？

王老师：都考。

大山：考不考汉字？

王老师：当然考。

大卫：是从第一课开始考吗？

王老师：是的，从第一课考到最后一课。

课文二　Text 2

（大家听到王老师在说考试的事情，都围拢过来。）

(People gather around when they hear Teacher Wang talking about the exam.)

安娜：王老师，下星期二考试难不难？

王老师：不太难。

莎莎：大家都能通过吗？

王老师：如果认真学习，一定能通过。

小米：王老师，考试几点开始？

王老师：八点开始，希望大家别迟到。

大山：考多长时间？

王老师：两个小时，十点结束。

（大家交完考卷。）

（After everyone hand in their papers.）

王老师：大家考得怎么样？

大山：还可以，只是觉得听力有点儿难。

安娜：我有几个词不太会写，其他都写上了。

小米：我觉得自己全部写上了。

王老师：真棒！

课文三　Text 3

快期末考试了，大家都很紧张。下课时，大家开始询问王老师有关考试的问题，王老师告诉大家，下星期二考试，考试时间是从 8 点到 10 点，共 2 个小时，提醒大家不要迟到。并且说，考试不太难，只要大家认真学习，都会通过的。

📝 生词 New Words

生　词	词　性	解　释	举　例
时候 shíhou	n	（the duration of）time；（a point in）time；moment	什么时候放假？ When is the holiday?
考 kǎo	vt	give/take an examination, a test or a quiz	我考了满分。 I got full marks in the exam.
考试 kǎoshì	n vt	examination, test, quiz；have/take an examination	我通过了考试。 I passed the exam.

生 词	词 性	解 释	举 例
下周 xiàzhōu	n	next week	下周见! See you next week!
教室 jiàoshì	n	classroom	进教室 enter the classroom
读写 dúxiě	n	speaking and writing	读写课 reading and writing class
听说 tīngshuō	n	listening and speaking	下周考试有听说和读写。 Next week's exam will include listening, speaking, and reading and writing.
从 cóng	prep	from	你从哪里来? Where are you from?
第 dì	auxili	auxiliary word for ordinal numbers	第三 third
课 kè	n	class; lesson	下课! Class is over!
第一课 dì yī kè		lesson One	
最后 zuìhòu	adj	final; last	从第一课到最后一课。 From the first lesson to the last lesson.
大家 dàjiā	pron	everyone	大家好! Hello everyone!
通过 tōngguò	vt	pass	通过考试 pass the exam
认真 rènzhēn	adv	seriously; earnestly	我考试的时候很认真。 I was very serious during the exam.
别 bié	aux	don't	别上当! Don't be fooled!
结束 jiéshù	v	finish	考试结束。 The exam is over.
汉字 hànzì	misc	Chinese characters	
期末 qīmò	n	end of term	期末考试 Final examination

续表

生 词	词 性	解 释	举 例
紧张 jǐnzhāng	adj	nervous	别紧张 take it easy; Don't be nervous
听力 tīnglì	n	listening	听力测试 listening test
希望 xīwàng	vt/n	hope; wish	我希望通过考试。 I hope to pass the exam.

汉字 Chinese Characters

独体字(dútǐzì)　Single character

大　

Its oracle script is 👤. The pictographic script symbolizes the form of a standing man.

末　

Its bronze script is 𣎵. The pictograph 木(mù，tree; wood)plus short horizontal stroke indicates the tree top.

后　

力　

Its oracle script is 𤣥. The pictographic script symbolizes the form of a farming tool for turning soil.

合体字(hétǐzì) Combined character

张　左右结构 zuǒyòu jiégòu　Left-right structure　弓　长

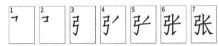

It is a signific-phonetic character. Its signific element is 弓(gōng, bow). Its phonetic element is 长(cháng, long; zhǎng, grow). Its primitive sense is to pull back the bow and shoot an arrow.

教　左右结构 zuǒyòu jiégòu　Left-right structure　孝　攵

Its oracle script is 𤕝, the right element is 攴(攵, pū). ┃ is teacher's ruler for beating pupils. 彐 is a hand. 攴 is holding a ruler in a hand. The left element 爻 means whole and broken linear symbols making up the eight trigrams in The Book of Changes. It Indicates the content of learning. 子(子) indicates a student or child. 𤕝 means to urge children to learn.

考　上下结构 shàngxià jiégòu　Upper-lower structure　耂　丂

Its oracle script is 耂. The pictograph describes an old man with a cane ┃.

Its primitive sense is old. An extended sense is to examine, e.g. 考试.

紧　上下结构 shàngxià jiégòu　Upper-lower structure　⺺　糸

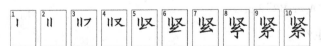

Its traditional Chinese character is written as 緊. The ideograph is composed of two elements：the upper element is 臤(qiān, firm; steady; hard; solid), and the other element is 糸（mì, thin silk thread）. Its primitive sense is the silk thread is tightly wound. An extended sense is nervous, e.g. 紧张.

家 上下结构 shàngxià jiégòu Upper-lower structure 宀 豕

Its oracle script is 𧱖. In the ideographical structure, ⌂ is a house, and 𧰧 is a pig. In ancient China, pig is one of the earliest domesticated animals in ancient China, and many families raised pigs in the house. It represents the characteristics of agricultural civilization.

最 上下结构 shàngxià jiégòu Upper-lower structure

The ideograph is composed of two elements: the upper element looks like a hat, and the lower element is 取（qǔ, take; get）. Its primitive sense is to offend and take away. A phonetic loaned sense is most; best; to the highest degree, e. g. 最好（best）; 最后（last）.

💬 语法 Grammar

连词"还是" The conjunction "还是"

汉语中用"还是"表示选择。一般来说，"还是"用在疑问句中可以构成"A 还是 B ？"例如：

In Chinese, "还是" is used to express choice. Generally speaking, "还是" can be used in interrogative sentences to form"A or B?"e.g.

1. A：他是老师还是学生？

   B：是老师。

2. A：你喝咖啡还是牛奶？

B：我喝咖啡。

3. A：考读写还是听说?

  B：都考。

固定格式"×不×" The fixed expression "×不×"

"×不×"格式是比较常见的一种反复问句格式。

动词 + 不 + 动词 + ?

The "×不×" format is a relatively common repeated question format.

Verb + 不 + Verb + ?

考不考?

买不买?

借不借?

说不说?

形容词 + 不 + 形容词 + ?

Adjective + 不 + Adjective + ?

难不难?

白不白?

好不好?

大不大?

📻 练习 Exercises

一、请听下面的词语选择对应的拼音 Listen and choose the correct pronunciation

1. ( ) A. kāoshì   B. kǎoshì   C. shíhou

2. ( ) A. nǎge   B. shénme   C. xīngqī

3. ( ) A. jiàoshì   B. lǎoshī   C. kǎoshì

4. ( ) A. dúxiě   B. dòuxiě   C. tīngshuō

5. ( ) A. hànzì   B. shàngkè   C. dìyī

6. ( ) A. shì   B. dìyī   C. zuìhòu

二、听后选择正确的图片 Listen and choose the right picture

A. B. C.

D. E. F.

G. H. I. J.

1. 考试(　　)　　　　2. 教室(　　)　　　　3. 汉字(　　)　　4. 听(　　　)

5. 读(　　)　　　　　6. 写(　　)　　　　　7. 真棒(　　)　　8. 老师(　　　)

9. 紧张(　　)　　　　10. 认真(　　)

三、选择所给词语的正确读音 Choose the correct pronunciation of the words given

1. (　　)时候　　A. shīhou　　　　B. shíhou　　　　C. shíhòu

2. (　　)下周　　A. xiàzhōu　　　B. xiàzhóu　　　C. xiāzhòu

3. (　　)从　　　A. cōng　　　　B. cón　　　　　C. cóng

4. (　　)最后　　A. zuìhòu　　　B. zìhòu　　　　C. zuīhōu

5. (　　)认真　　A. rènzhēng　　B. rènzhēn　　　C. rénzhēn

6. (　　)结束　　A. jiésù　　　　B. jiéshù　　　　C. jiěshù

四、请用下列词语填空 Please fill in the blanks with the following words

A. 考试　　B. 叫　　C. 还可以　　D. 下课时　　E. 还是　　F. 哪个

G. 学习

例如：我(B)大山。

1. (　　)我们什么时候_____？

2. (　　)考读写_____听说？

3. (　　)在_____教室考试？

4. (　　)A：你考试考得怎么样？

　　　B：_____，只是觉得听力有点难。

198

5. （　　）如果认真_____，一定能通过考试。

6. （　　）_____，大家开始询问王老师有关考试的问题

五、汉字练习 Chinese character practice

1. 找出现代汉字对应的古代汉字 Match the ancient Chinese characters and the modern Chinese characters

大　　　　　　　勢

末　　　　　　　大

家　　　　　　　末

教　　　　　　　身

2. 分析下列汉字的结构 Analyze the structure of the following Chinese characters

通　考　过　写　第　最　认　别

左右结构 Left-right structure _____

上下结构 Upper-lower structure _____

左下包围结构 Left-lower surrounding structure _____

3. 写出下列汉字的笔画 Write the strokes of the following Chinese characters

候_____

试_____

周_____

室_____

读_____

写_____

六、书写练习 Writing exercises

1. 按正确的顺序组合句子并书写在横线上 Assemble the sentences in the correct order and write them on the line

例如：叫　我　大山

我叫大山。

(1)什么　　老师　　们　　时候　　我　　考试？

_____

(2)考　　第一　　吗　　开始　　从　　课　　是？

_____

(3)星期　　难　　王老师　　的　　二　　不难　　考试？

_____

(4)通过　　能　　大家　　都　　吗？

_____

(5)开始　　几点　　王　　考试　　老师？

_____

(6)时　　多　　长　　间　　考？

_____

2. 书写汉字 Writing Chinese characters

例如：我 jiào（叫）小米。

(1)下 Xīngqī（　　　　　）二考试。

(2)考 dúxiě（　　　　　）还是听说？

(3)是的，从第一 kè（　　　　　）考到最后一课。

(4)王老师，下星期二 kǎoshì（　　　　　）难不难？

(5)如果认真 xuéxí（　　　　　），一定能通过。

(6)王老师，考试几点 kāishǐ（　　　　　）？

七、课堂活动 Class activities

两人一组，分别扮演老师和同学，询问考试时间、地点及其难易程度等情况。

In groups of two, play the role of a teacher and a classmate, respectively, and ask about the time, place and difficulty of the exam.

第二十课　你什么时候回国?

Lesson 20　When will you return to your country?

📅 课文 Text

课文一　Text 1

在留学生元旦联欢会上，一明和大江遇到大山和小米，询问大山和小米回国时间。

At the New Year's Day party for international students, Yi Ming and Da Jiang meet Da Shan and Xiao Mi, they ask when Da Shan and Xiao Mi will come back home.

（一明和大江找到大山和小米，四人围坐一起。）

（Yi Ming and Da Jiang find Da Shan and Xiao Mi, and the four of them sit together in a circle.）

一明：你们寒假都要回国吧?

小米：是的，大山要和我一起回英国。你们呢?

一明：我们马上毕业了，要留在学校写毕业论文。

小米：真辛苦啊!

一明：你们什么时候回国?

小米：我们打算期末考试一结束就走。

一明：买机票了吗?

小米：已经买了。

一明：买的是什么时候?

小米：是一月十五日的票。

一明：哦，快要到了。

小米：是的，大概还有两周时间。

课文二　Text 2

（大江在一旁插话。）

（Da Jiang interjects from the side.）

大江：你们怎么去机场？

大山：我们打算乘地铁去。

大江：哦，挺方便的。

一明：从学校到机场乘地铁需要多长时间？

小米：大概需要一个半小时。

一明：挺远的。早点儿出发，别迟到了。

小米：好的。谢谢。

大江：从北京到英国伦敦需要多长时间？

小米：快的话，需要 8 个多小时；慢的话，需要 20 多个小时。

大江：回国后，别忘了，微信联系。

小米：好的，微信联系。虽然这次回国时间有点儿长，但是我们常联系。

一明：好，祝你们一路平安。

课文三　Text 3

寒假马上快到了，在元旦联欢晚会上，一明和大江找到小米和大山。

小米和大山期末考试结束就回国，大山要去小米的家。两个人买的是一月十五号的票，还有两周就出发了。

两个人要乘地铁到机场，路上大概需要花一个半小时时间。从北京到英国伦敦乘飞机，最快需要 8 个多小时，最慢需要 20 多个小时。

一明和大江，因为要写毕业论文，不回家，要留在学校。

四人相约，寒假要经常微信联系。

📝 生词 New Words

生　词	词　性	解　释	举　例
回国 huí guó		return to one's country	你什么时候回国？ When will you back to your country?
寒假 hánjià	n	winter vacation；winter holiday	寒假快到了。 The winter vacation is coming.
毕业 bìyè	vi	graduate	大学毕业 graduated from college
留在 liúzài	vt	stay at/in	留在家里 stay at home
学校 xuéxiào	n	school	留在学校 stay at school
论文 lùnwén	n	paper；thesis	写论文 write a paper
辛苦 xīnkǔ	adj	hard；laborious；toilsome	上班很辛苦。 It's hard to go to work.
真辛苦 zhēn xīnkǔ		really exhausted；really hard	爬山真辛苦。 It's really hard to climb the mountain.
打算 dǎsuàn	vt	intend；plan	她打算留在学校写毕业论文。 She plans to stay at school and write her graduation thesis.
机票 jīpiào	n	airline ticket	订机票 book a plane ticket
机场 jīchǎng	n	airport	我到机场了。 I arrived at the airport.
将近 jiāngjìn	adv	nearly；almost	这顿饭将近 600 元。 This meal costs nearly 600 yuan.

生　词	词　性	解　释	举　例
两周 liǎng zhōu		fortnight；two weeks	我有两周的假期。 I have a two-week vacation.
路上 lù shang		on the road；on the way	我在回家的路上。 I am on my way home.
挺 tǐng	adv	very；quite；pretty；rather	地铁挺快的。 The subway is very fast.
乘 chéng	vi	ride；take；by	乘公交车 by bus 乘火车 take the train 乘飞机 by air
地铁 dìtiě	n	subway	坐地铁 take the subway
需要 xūyào	n；vt	need；want	我需要你的帮助。 I need your help.
大概 dàgài	adv	probably；roughly	礼物大概明天能到。 The gift will probably arrive tomorrow.
远 yuǎn	adj	distant	南极很远。 Antarctica is far away.
伦敦 lúndūn	n	London	从北京到伦敦大概有多远？ How far is it from Beijing to London?
忘 wàng	vt	forget	别忘记我。 Don't forget me.
常 cháng	adv	often	我常跑步。 I often run.
联系 liánxì	vt	contact；touch	别忘了，常联系！ Don't forget to keep in touch！
次 cì	quant	time in repetition	第一次 first time

续表

生 词	词 性	解 释	举 例
这次 zhè cì		this time; present; current:	这次我很满意。 I am very satisfield this time.
最快 zuì kuài		fastest	飞机是最快的。 Airplanes are the fastest.
最慢 zuì màn		slowest	谁是最慢的？ Who is the slowest?
元旦 yuándàn	n	New Year's Day	元旦快乐！ Happy New Year's Day!
联欢晚会 lián huān wǎnhuì	n	party; gathering; evening party	元旦联欢晚会 New Year's Eve party
祝 zhù	vt	wish	祝你好运。 Wish you good luck.
一路平安 yī lù píngān		May you be safe throughout the journey	祝你一路平安！ Have a safe trip！

汉字 Chinese Characters

独体字(dútǐzì) Single character

元　一　二　亓　元

Its bronze script is 𠘧. The pictographic script highlights a person's head. Its primitive sense is head, and an extended sense is start; beginning. 元旦(New year's Day)is the first day of each year in the Gregorian calendar. It is the beginning of the year.

旦　

Its oracle script is ⊖. It is an indicative character, the upper element is the sun, and the lower element represents ground. It indicates the sun has just risen from the ground. Its primitive sense is dawn; daybreak.

合体字(hétǐzì)　Combined character

寒　上下结构 shàngxià jiégòu　Upper-lower structure

Its small seal script is 寒, In the ideographical structure, the outer element is a house ∩, the inner elements look like a person is surrounded by straw Ψ, but he still feels cold, the element 仌 is (bīng, ice; feel cold). Its primitive sense is cold.

安　上下结构 shàngxià jiégòu　Upper-lower structure　宀　女

Its oracle script is 安. The ideograph is composed of two pictographic elements: ∩ (mián) means a house, 女 means a woman. Its primitive sense is safe.

忘　上下结构 shàngxià jiégòu　Upper-lower structure　亡　心

It is a signific-phonetic character. It is also an ideograph. Its signific element is 心(xīn, heart; mind; feeling). Its phonetic element is 亡(wáng, lose; be gone). Its primitive sense is to forget.

假　左右结构 zuǒyòu jiégòu　Left-right structure　亻　叚

It is a signific-phonetic character. Its signific element is 亻(人, rén, person). Its phonetic element is 叚(jiǎ, lose; be gone). Its primitive sense is to borrow.

联　左右结构 zuǒyòu jiégòu　Left-right structure　耳　关

Its oracle script is ☒. The ideograph is composed of two pictographic elements. The left element ☒ is 耳(ěr, ear; any ear-like thing) which refers to the ears on ancient bronzes. The right element ☒ is 丝(sī, silk). It describes connecting the ears of bronzes with wires which means connecting, e. g. 联系(keep in contact with).

语法 Grammar

介词"从"　The preposition "从"

介词"从"表示起点，后接处所词、方位词、时间词，常与"到、往、向"等搭配使用，表示事情的发展、变化。

The preposition "从" indicates the starting point, followed by the word of place, location, and time. It is often used in conjunction with "到(to)，往(to)，向(to)", etc., to indicate the development and change of things.

从 + 处所词

从 + Place Noun

1. 从图书馆到食堂。

2. 从北京到上海，坐飞机要两个多小时。

3. 从我家到学校不太远。

从+方位词，例如：

1. 从上到下，都是黑颜色。

2. 从里到外，都很漂亮。

3. 从东到西，有 200 米远。

从 + 时间词

从 + Time Noun，e.g.

1. 从 8 点到 10 点上课。

2. 从 15 岁到 20 岁。

3. 从第三课到第五课。

"一……就……" The correlative "一……就……"

"一……就……"连接一个复句。

"一……就……"links a complex sentence to indicate.

表示后一动作紧跟着前一动作发生。例如：

The second act immediately follows the first act，e.g.

1. 今天一下课，我们就去食堂吃饭。

2. 我一到中国就给妈妈打电话。

3. 我们打算期末考试一结束就走。

表示前一动作是条件和原因，后一动作是结果。例如：

The first act is the condition or the cause of the second act，e.g.

1. 中国人一听就知道你是外国人。

2. 我一到冬天就感冒。

3. 汉语我一学就会。

练习 Exercises

一、请听下面的词语选择对应的拼音 Listen and choose the correct pronunciation

1. (　　) A. hán jià 　　 B. huí guó 　　 C. dōu yào

2. (　　) A. bìyè 　　 B. liúzài 　　 C. hán jià

3. (　　) A. xuéxiào 　　 B. xīnkǔ 　　 C. lùnwén

4. (　　) A. zhēn xīnkǔ 　　 B. dōu yào 　　 C. huí guó

5. (　　) A. dǎsuàn 　　 B. jīchǎng 　　 C. jīpiào

6. (　　) A. liǎng zhōu 　　 B. jiāngjìn 　　 C. lù shang

二、听后选择正确的图片 Listen and choose the right picture

A. 　B. 　C. 　D.

E. 　F. 　G. 　H.

I. 　J.

1. 伦敦(　　)　2. 地铁(　　)　3. 微信(　　)　4. 毕业(　　)　5. 机场(　　)

6. 联欢晚会(　　) 7. 元旦(　　)　8. 机票(　　)　9. 学校(　　)　10. 论文(　　)

三、选择所给词语的正确读音 Choose the correct pronunciation of the words given

1. (　　)这次　　A. zhé cī　　　B. zhē cī　　　C. zhè cì

2. (　　)最快　　A. zuì kuà　　B. zuì kuài　　C. zù kuài

3. (　　)元旦　　A. yuándàn　　B. yuāndàn　　C. yándàn

4. (　　)祝　　　A. zhù　　　　B. zhú　　　　C. zhū

5. (　　)平安　　A. pínān　　　B. pīngān　　　C. píngān

6. (　　)晚会　　A. wánhuì　　B. wǎnhuì　　　C. wánhui

四、请用下列词语填空 Please fill in the blanks with the following words

A. 乘　　B. 叫　　C. 怎么　　D. 需要　　E. 打算　　F. 好的　　G. 一路平安

例如：我(B)大山。

1. (　　)我们_____期末考试结束后就走。

2. (　　)你们_____去机场？

3. (　　)我们打算_____地铁去。

4. (　　)从学校到机场乘地铁_____多长时间？

5. (　　)祝你们_____。

6. (　　)A：挺远的。早点出发，别迟到。

　　　 B：_____。谢谢。

209

五、汉字练习 Chinese character practice

1. 找出现代汉字对应的古代汉字 Match the ancient Chinese characters and the modern Chinese characters

文

元

联

安

旦

2. 分析下列汉字的结构 Analyze the structure of the following Chinese characters

周　远　机　近　回　国

左下包围结构 Lower-left surrounding structure_____

左右结构 Left-right structure _____

全包围结构 Complete surrounding structure_____

上三包围结构 Left-top-right surrounding structure_____

3. 写出下列汉字的笔画 Write the strokes of the following Chinese characters

辛_____

苦_____

地_____

铁_____

联_____

系_____

六、书写练习 Writing exercises

1. 按正确的顺序组合句子并书写在横线上 Assemble the sentences in the correct order and write them on the line

例如：叫　我　大山

我叫大山。

(1)苦　啊　辛　真！

_____

(2) 吗　票　机　买　了？

_____

(3) 地铁　打算　我们　乘　去。

_____

(4) 快　了　马上　寒假　到

_____

(5) 家　的　大山　去　小米　要

_____

(6) 时间　大概　小时　需要　路上　花　一个半

_____

2. 书写汉字 Writing Chinese characters

例如：我 jiào（叫）小米。

(1) 你们寒假都要 huí guó（　　　　）吧？

(2) 我们马上 bìyè（　　　　）了，要留在学校写毕业论文。

(3) 真 xīnkǔ（　　　　）啊！

(4) 买 jīpiào（　　　　）了吗？

(5) 你们怎么去 jīchǎng（　　　　）？

(6) 是的，还有将近 liǎng zhōu（　　　　）的时间。

七、课堂活动 Class activities

两人一组，互相询问寒假安排，比如回家，机票购买、路上行程、怎么去车站等情况进行会话。

In groups of two, ask each other about winter vacation arrangements, such as going home, air ticket purchase, itinerary, how to get to the station, etc. to have a conversation.

生词索引表

生　词	拼　音	课　文
A		
1. 啊	à	10
B		
2. 吧	ba	8
3. 半	bàn	7
4. 半小时	bànxiǎoshí	9
5. 帮助	bāngzhù	14
6. 比较	bǐjiào	14
7. 毕业	bìyè	20
8. 别	bié	19
9. 不	bù	2
10. 不错	búcuò	14
11. 不但	bùdàn	14
12. 不急	bù jí	10
13. 不客气	bú kèqi	18
14. 不是	búshì	2
15. 不同	bùtóng	4
C		
16. 才	cái	5

生　词	拼　音	课　文
17. 菜鸟驿站	Càiniǎo Yìzhàn	15
18. 称呼	chēnghu	1
19. 差	chà	9
20. 差不多	chàbuduō	14
21. 常	cháng	20
22. 乘	chéng	20
23. 吃	chī	7
24. 吃饭	chī fàn	7
25. 迟到	chídào	16
26. 尺寸	chǐcùn	11
27. 出去	chūqù	16
28. 穿	chuān	11
29. 次	cì	20
30. 从	cóng	19
D		
31. 打算	dǎsuàn	20
32. 大	dà	3
33. 大概	dàgài	20
34. 大家	dàjiā	19
35. 大小	dàxiǎo	11
36. 带	dài	15
37. 但是	dànshì	6
38. 当然	dāngrán	14
39. 到	dào	15
40. 打折	dǎzhé	12
41. 的	de	1

续表

生　词	拼　音	课　文
42. 得	de	18
43. 登录	dēnglù	14
44. 等	děng	9
45. 第	dì	19
46. 第一课	dì yī kè	19
47. 地方	dìfang	15
48. 地铁	dìtiě	20
49. 点	diǎn	7
50. 点儿	diǎnr	18
51. 电话	diànhuà	10
52. 电影	diànyǐng	9
53. 电影院	diànyǐngyuàn	9
54. 店员	diànyuán	12
55. 都	dōu	4
56. 东西	dōngxi	10
57. 懂	dǒng	18
58. 读	dú	17
59. 读写	dúxiě	19
60. 度	dù	18
61. 短信	duǎnxìn	15
62. 对不起	duì bu qǐ	10
63. 多	duō	3
64. 多长	duō cháng	17
65. 多大	duō dà	11
E		
66. 而且	érqiě	14

续表

生　词	拼　音	课　文
F		
67. 发音	fāyīn	17
68. 法国	Fǎguó	2
69. 饭	fàn	7
70. 方便	fāngbiàn	13
71. 方式	fāngshì	13
72. 放	fàng	10
73. 法国人	Fǎguó rén	2
74. 非常	fēicháng	11
75. 非常感谢	fēicháng gǎnxiè	18
76. 粉色	fěnsè	11
77. 风	fēng	6
78. 服装店	fúzhuāngdiàn	12
79. 付款	fùkuǎn	13
G		
80. 敢	gǎn	18
81. 感觉	gǎnjué	14
82. 感冒	gǎnmào	18
83. 感谢	gǎnxiè	18
84. 干什么	gàn shénme	10
85. 高	gāo	18
86. 高烧	gāoshāo	18
87. 告诉	gàosù	14
88. 刚	gāng	12
89. 个	gè	3
90. 给	gěi	10

续表

生　词	拼　音	课　文
91. 公园	gōngyuán	8
92. 国	guó	2
93. 国家	guójiā	17
94. 过	guò	17
95. 贵	guì	12
H		
96. 还	hái	9
97. 还差	hái　chà	9
98. 还是	háishi	6
99. 海门	Hǎimén	18
100. 寒假	hánjià	20
101. 汉语	hànyǔ	17
102. 汉字	hànzì	19
103. 号	hào	11
104. 喝	hē	18
105. 和	hé	7
106. 合适	héshì	12
107. 很	hěn	9
108. 很好	hěn hǎo	9
109. 喉咙	hóulóng	18
110. 后	hòu	12
111. 后来	hòulái	12
112. 花	huā	12
113. 化妆品	huàzhuāngpǐn	14
114. 欢迎	huānyíng	1
115. 欢迎下次光临	huānyíng xiàcì guānglín	13

生 词	拼 音	课 文
116. 还	huán	9
117. 还书	huán shū	9
118. 回国	huí guó	20
119. 回去	huíqù	18
120. 会	huì	15
121. 或者	huòzhě	13
J		
122. 机场	jīchǎng	20
123. 机票	jīpiào	20
124. 急	jí	10
125. 几	jǐ	3
126. 几点	jǐ diǎn	7
127. 几楼	jǐ lóu	7
128. 几岁	jǐ suì	3
129. 计算机	jìsuànjī	4
130. 计算机专业	jìsuànjī zhuānyè	4
131. 价格	jiàgé	12
132. 简单	jiǎndān	14
133. 件	jiàn	11
134. 建筑	jiànzhù	4
135. 建筑专业	jiànzhù zhuānyè	4
136. 将近	jiāngjìn	20
137. 教	jiāo	14
138. 交通专业	jiāotōng zhuānyè	4
139. 叫	jiào	1
140. 教室	jiàoshì	19

续表

生　词	拼　音	课　文
141. 家人	jiāren	3
142. 接	jiē	10
143. 接电话	jiē diànhuà	10
144. 接下来	jiēxiàlái	14
145. 结束	jiéshù	19
146. 借书	jiè shū	9
147. 今年	jīnnián	3
148. 今天	jīntiān	8
149. 紧张	jǐnzhāng	19
150. 京东	Jīngdōng	14
151. 静音	jìngyīn	10
152. 就	jiù	11
153. 据说	jùshuō	9
154. 觉得	juéde	17
K		
155. 开始	kāishǐ	9
156. 砍价	kǎn jià	12
157. 看	kàn	6
158. 看病	kàn bìng	18
159. 看看	kànkan	15
160. 看中	kànzhòng	12
161. 考	kǎo	19
162. 考试	kǎoshì	19
163. 可能	kěnéng	16
164. 可以	kěyǐ	6
165. 课	kè	19

生　词	拼　音	课　文
166. 快	kuài	9
167. 快递	kuàidì	14
168. 快递员	kuàidìyuán	15
L		
169. 来	lái	5
170. 了	le	5
171. 联欢晚会	lián huān wǎnhuì	20
172. 联系	liánxì	20
173. 两个	liǎng gè	14
174. 两周	liǎng zhōu	20
175. 留学	liúxué	5
176. 留学生	liúxuéshēng	18
177. 留在	liúzài	20
178. 楼	lóu	7
179. 楼下	lóu xià	10
180. 路上	lù shang	20
181. 伦敦	Lúndūn	20
182. 论文	lùnwén	20
M		
183. 吗	ma	1
184. 妈妈	māma	3
185. 马上	mǎshàng	16
186. 买	mǎi	10
187. 卖	mài	12
188. 慢慢儿	mànmānr	10
189. 忙	máng	14

生　词	拼　音	课　文
190. 没	méi	6
191. 没关系	méi guānxi	6
192. 没问题	méi wèntí	18
193. 没有	méiyǒu	6
194. 美国	Měiguó	2
195. 美国人	Měiguó rén	2
196. 们	men	1
197. 明白	míngbai	5
198. 明天	míngtiān	8
199. 名字	míngzi	1
N		
200. 哪	nǎ	2
201. 哪个	nǎge	7
202. 哪里	nǎli	10
203. 哪儿	nǎr	8
204. 那	nà	11
205. 难	nán	17
206. 哪些	nǎxiē	13
207. 呢	ne	4
208. 能	néng	12
209. 你	nǐ	1
210. 你好	nǐ hǎo	1
211. 你们	nǐmen	1
212. 年纪	niánjì	3
213. 您	nín	1
214. 弄	nòng	14

生　词	拼　音	课　文
215. 女儿	nǚ ér	3
O		
216. 哦	ò	5
P		
217. 旁边	pángbiān	15
218. 陪	péi	18
219. 便宜	piányi	12
220. 漂亮	piàoliang	11
221. 苹果	píngguǒ	15
Q		
222. 期末	qīmò	19
223. 起床	qǐ chuáng	16
224. 前	qián	17
225. 晴天	qíngtiān	6
226. 请假	qǐng jià	16
227. 请问	qǐng wèn	1
228. 取	qǔ	14
229. 去	qù	8
230. 裙子	qúnzi	11
R		
231. 人	rén	2
232. 认真	rènzhēn	19
233. 容易	róngyì	17
234. 如果	rúguǒ	13
235. 软件	ruǎnjiàn	14

续表

生　词	拼　音	课　文
	S	
236. 三个月	sān gè yuè	17
237. 扫	sǎo	13
238. 上课	shàng kè	16
239. 上午	shàngwǔ	6
240. 稍等	shāo děng	11
241. 少	shǎo	7
242. 谁	shuí	3
243. 什么	shénme	1
244. 生病	shēngbìng	16
245. 时间	shíjiān	17
246. 时候	shíhou	19
247. 食堂	shítáng	7
248. 是	shì	1
249. 是的	shìde	1
250. 适合	shìhé	11
251. 试试	shìshi	11
252. 试一下	shì yīxià	18
253. 事情	shìqing	8
254. 收到	shōudào	15
255. 收货人	shōuhuò rén	15
256. 手机短信	shǒujī duǎnxìn	15
257. 手机号	shǒujī hào	15
258. 蔬菜	shūcài	14
259. 舒服	shūfu	18

续表

生　　词	拼　　音	课　　文
260. 水	shuǐ	18
261. 水果	shuǐguǒ	14
262. 睡觉	shuìjiào	16
263. 说	shuō	6
264. 四位	sì wèi	15
265. 虽然	suīrán	6
266. 岁	suì	3
T		
267. 他们	tāmen	4
268. 太	tài	6
269. 淘宝	Táobǎo	14
270. 疼	téng	18
271. 体温	tǐwēn	18
272. 天气	tiānqì	6
273. 天气预报	tiānqì yùbào	6
274. 听见	tīngjiàn	10
275. 听力	tīnglì	19
276. 听说	tīngshuō	19
277. 挺	tǐng	20
278. 通过	tōngguò	19
279. 通知	tōngzhī	15
280. 痛	tòng	16
281. 同	tóng	4
282. 头	tóu	16
283. 图书馆	túshūguǎn	9

续表

生 词	拼 音	课 文
W		
284. 晚上	wǎnshang	9
285. 玩	wán	8
286. 玩儿	wánr	8
287. 网购	wǎnggòu	14
288. 网上	wǎngshàng	14
289. 忘	wàng	20
290. 微信	Wēixìn	13
291. 微信码	Wēixìnmǎ	13
292. 为什么	wèi shénme	5
293. 文化	wénhuà	5
294. 我	wǒ	1
295. 我们	wǒmen	4
X		
296. 希望	xīwàng	19
297. 喜欢	xǐhuan	5
298. 下次	xiàcì	16
299. 下来	xiàlái	10
300. 下午	xiàwǔ	6
301. 下载	xiàzài	14
302. 下周	xiàzhōu	19
303. 现金	xiànjīn	13
304. 现在	xiànzài	7
305. 小	xiǎo	11
306. 小时	xiǎoshí	9

续表

生　词	拼　音	课　文
307. 相同	xiāngtóng	4
308. 想	xiǎng	10
309. 写	xiě	17
310. 谢谢	xièxie	1
311. 休息	xiūxi	18
312. 辛苦	xīnkǔ	20
313. 星期	xīngqī	8
314. 星期几	xīngqī jǐ	8
315. 星期五	Xīngqīwǔ	8
316. 星期六	Xīngqīliù	8
317. 行	xíng	18
318. 姓名	xìngmíng	15
319. 需要	xūyào	20
320. 学	xué	17
321. 学过	xuéguò	17
322. 学习	xuéxí	14
323. 学校	xuéxiào	20
Y		
324. 呀	yā, ya	3
325. 要	yào	16
326. 药	yào	18
327. 钥匙	yàoshi	10
328. 也	yě	4
329. 一点儿	yìdiǎnr	9
330. 一定	yídìng	16

续表

生　词	拼　音	课　文
331. 衣服	yīfu	11
332. 一会儿	yíhuìr	7
333. 一件	yíjiàn	12
334. 一路平安	yí lù píngān	20
335. 一起	yìqǐ	8
336. 医生	yīshēng	16
337. 一食堂	yī shítáng	7
338. 一下儿	yíxiàr	9
339. 医院	yīyuàn	16
340. 阴天	yīntiān	6
341. 因为	yīnwèi	5
342. 应该	yīng gāi	7
343. 英国	Yīngguó	2
344. 英国人	Yīngguó rén	2
345. 用	yòng	13
346. 有	yǒu	8
347. 有点儿	yǒudiǎnr	11
348. 雨	yǔ	6
349. 预报	yùbào	6
350. 元	yuán	12
351. 元旦	yuándàn	20
352. 原来	yuánlái	17
353. 远	yuǎn	20
354. 院	yuàn	9
355. 月	yuè	17

生　词	拼　音	课　文
Z		
356. 在	zài	10
357. 再	zài	12
358. 再见	zàijiàn	17
359. 早饭	zǎofàn	16
360. 怎么	zěnme	1
361. 怎么办	zěnme bàn	14
362. 怎么样	zěnmeyàng	11
363. 找	zhǎo	10
364. 找到	zhǎodào	10
365. 照片	zhàopiàn	3
366. 这	zhè	3
367. 这次	zhècì	20
368. 这位	zhèwèi	3
369. 真	zhēn	14
370. 真棒	zhēn bàng	17
371. 真辛苦	zhēn xīnkǔ	20
372. 正	zhèng	11
373. 正好	zhènghǎo	11
374. 正在	zhèngzài	16
375. 知道	zhīdào	10
376. 支付宝	Zhīfùbǎo	13
377. 只	zhǐ	17
378. 只要	zhǐyào	15
379. 中国	Zhōngguó	5

续表

生　词	拼　音	课　文
380. 中国文化	Zhōngguó wénhuà	5
381. 中国银行	Zhōngguó yínháng	15
382. 祝	zhù	20
383. 注册	zhùcè	14
384. 注意	zhùyì	15
385. 专业	zhuānyè	4
386. 自己	zìjǐ	13
387. 最后	zuìhòu	19
388. 最快	zuì kuài	20
389. 最慢	zuì màn	20

参考文献

[1][荷]艾布拉姆·德·斯旺. 世界上的语言：全球语言系统[M]. 广州：花城出版社，2008.

[2][美]爱德华·萨丕尔. 语言论[M]. 陆卓元，译. 陆志韦，校订. 北京：商务印书馆，1985.

[3]陈绥宁. 基础汉语40课（上）[M]. 上海：华东师范大学出版社，2003.

[4]陈绥宁. 基础汉语40课（下）[M]. 上海：华东师范大学出版社，2003.

[5]顾嘉祖. 跨文化交际——外国语言文学中的隐蔽文化[M]. 南京：南京师范大学出版社，2000.

[6]国家对外汉语教学领导小组办公室. 高等学校外国留学生汉语言专业教学大纲[M]. 北京：北京语言大学出版社，2002.

[7]国家对外汉语教学领导小组办公室汉语水平考试部，刘英林. 汉语水平等级标准与语法等级大纲[M]. 北京：高等教育出版社，1996.

[8]应晨锦. 国际中文教育中文水平等级标准：语法学习手册（初等）[M]. 北京：北京语言大学出版社，2022.

[9]应晨锦，王鸿滨，金海月，等. 国际中文教育中文水平等级标准：语法学习手册（高等）[M]. 北京：北京语言大学出版社，2022.

[10]应晨锦，王鸿滨，金海月，等. 国际中文教育中文水平等级标准：语法学习手册（中等）[M]. 北京：北京语言大学出版社，2022.

[11]胡附，文炼. 现代汉语语法探索[M]. 北京：新知识出版社，1956.

[12]胡壮麟. 语言学教程[M]. 3版. 北京：北京大学出版社，2006.

[13]黄建华，陈楚祥. 双语词典学导论[M]. 北京：商务印书馆，1997.

[14]教育部中外语言交流合作中心. 国际中文教育中文水平等级标准[M]. 北京：北京语言大学出版社，2021.

[15]康玉华，来思平. 汉语会话301句[M]. 范建民，刘京玉，译. 北京：北京语言学院出版社，1990.

[16]孔子学院总部/国家汉办. 国际汉语教学通用课程大纲[M]. 北京：外语教学与研究出版社，2008.

[17]李临定. 现代汉语句型[M]. 北京：商务印书馆，2011.

[18]李泉. 对外汉语教材研究[M]. 北京：商务印书馆，2006.

[19]李晓琪，任雪梅，徐晶凝. 博雅汉语（初级·起步篇）[M]. 北京：北京大学出版社，2004.

[20]刘德联，刘晓雨. 中级汉语口语[M]. 2版. 北京：北京大学出版社，2004.

[21]刘珣. 对外汉语教育学引论[M]. 北京：北京语言文化大学出版社，2000.

[22]刘月华，等. 实用现代汉语语法[M]. 2版. 北京：商务印书馆，2001.

[23]陆俭明. "对外汉语教学"中的语法教学[J]. 语言教学与研究，2000(3).

[24]吕叔湘. 中国文法要略[M]. 北京：商务印书馆，1956.

[25]吕文华. 关于对外汉语教学语法体系的若干问题[J]. 海外华文教育，2002(3).

[26]潘文国. 汉英语言对比概论[M]. 北京：商务印书馆，2010.

[27]荣继华. 发展汉语（初级综合）[M]. 北京：北京语言大学出版社，2011.

[28]谭载喜. 奈达论翻译[M]. 北京：中国对外翻译出版公司，1984.

[29]王还. 对外汉语教学语法大纲[M]. 北京：北京语言学院出版社，1995.

[30]王力. 中国现代语法[M]. 北京：商务印书馆，1985.

[31]徐品香. 对外汉语教学词语英文译释研究[M]. 北京：人民邮电出版社，2013.

[32]杨寄洲. 汉语教程（第二册　下）[M]. 3版. 北京：北京语言大学出版社，2016.

[33]中国社会科学院. 现代汉语词典[M]. 7版. 北京：商务印书馆，2023.

[34]钟梫. 钟梫对外汉语教学初探[M]. 北京：北京语言大学出版社，2006.

[35]周小兵，李海鸥. 对外汉语教学入门[M]. 广州：中山大学出版社，2004.

[36]朱勇，等. 爱上中国[M]. 北京：外语教学与研究出版社，2011.

[37]Allen J M, Muragishi G A, Smith J L, et al. To grab and to hold：Cultivating communal goals to overcome cultural and structural barriers in first-generation college students' science interest[J]. Translational Issues in Psychological Science, 2015.

[38]Bloom K C, Shuell T J. Effects of massed and distributed practice on the learning and retention of second-language vocabulary[J]. Journal of Educational Research, 1981.

[39]Boulding K. The Image[M]. Ann Arbor：University of Michigan Press, 1956.

[40]Cao F, Vu M, Chan H, et al. Writing affects the brain network of reading in Chinese：An fMRI study[J]. Human Brain Mapping, 2013.

[41]Grant A M, Berry J W. The necessity of others is the mother of invention：Intrinsic and

prosocial motivations, perspective taking, and creativity [J]. Academy of Management Journal, 2011.

[42] Gelb, Ignace J. A Study of Writing[M]. Chicago: University of Chicago Press, 1963.

[43] Lam H C. A critical analysis of the various ways for teaching Chinese characters [J]. Electronic Journal of Foreign Language Teaching, 2011.

[44] Means. Way[J]. Structure, 2002(4).

[45] Nida E A, Taber C R. The theory and practice of [Biblical] translation [M]. Leiden: Brill, 1969.

[46] Xu Y, Chang L-Y, Zhang J, et al. Reading, writing, and animation in character learning in Chinese as a foreign language[J]. Foreign Language Annals, 2013.

[47] Zhang Wangxi, Liu Runqing. A Summary of the Forum on Language Learning Theory— Editing Board of Chinese Teaching in the World Editing Board of Applied Linguistics Editing Board of Language Teaching and Linguistic Studies[J]. 世界汉语教学, 1992, 6(4).